WEEKEND COOK

100 Sensational Dishes for the Cook in a Hurry

WEEKEND COOK

100 Sensational Dishes for the Cook in a Hurry

· EVELYN ROSE & SULA LEON ·

PIATKUS

To our husbands, Myer Rose and Anthony Leon,
for their boundless patience, support – and love.

First published in 1994 by
Judy Piatkus (Publishers) Ltd
5 Windmill Street,
London W1P 1HF

The moral rights of the authors have been asserted

A catalogue record for this book is available from the British Library

ISBN 0-7499-1420-3

Edited by Susan Fleming
Designed by Jerry Goldie
Photography by Martin Brigdale
Illustrations by Madeleine Thompson

Typeset by Phoenix Photosetting, Chatham, Kent
Printed and bound in Great Britain by
Butler & Tanner, Frome and London

Contents

Introduction

During the twelve years that we have been conducting our Master Classes for Creative Cooks, the 'profile' of the people attending has remained very much the same, the factor common to all being a passionate interest in food and its use in elegant home cooking.

What has changed, however, is the amount of time and effort they are prepared to invest in what can be an all-consuming occupation. In the last five years, for example, we have noticed that the sessions most heavily subscribed were those that promised exciting results with the minimum of effort. Titles like 'Simple but Sophisticated', 'Entertaining à la Minute' and 'Simply Special' have been greeted with enthusiasm by even the most dedicated aficionados of what the French call 'cuisine soignée' – that is, cooking as a domestic as opposed to a professional art form.

In this book we have distilled the best of these sessions. However, we have not made speed our first priority – you may well find dishes elsewhere that are even faster to prepare. Instead we set out to devise dishes that combine ease of preparation with the highest degree of satisfaction for both the eye and the palate.

What has made it possible to take most of the strain out of what might be called 'hobby' cooking is the change of emphasis from technique to ingredients. Now much of the excitement of cooking can be found in the use of what were once considered 'exotic' foods – foods that a few years ago needed a pilgrimage to a distant deli or ethnic food shop, but are now increasingly to be found on the shelves of the local supermarket. The list is almost endless: wine vinegars flavoured with herbs; single-estate extra virgin olive oils; Provençale garlic and vine-ripened tomatoes; fresh herbs by the bunch; Mediterranean fish such as fresh tuna and sea bass; kumquats from Israel and mangoes from Brazil; not to mention the 'home-grown' goods such as free-range eggs and poultry, 'organic' meats and miniature asparagus. There are also the newly 'fashionable' foods such as goat's cheese and sun-dried tomatoes, rocket and lamb's lettuce, 'wild' mushrooms and butternut squash, fresh ginger and jasmine rice.

An even newer development of interest for the dedicated cook in a hurry is the growing number of 'convenience' ingredients where the tedious part of the preparation is done at the food factory, leaving only the pleasurable part to be done in the home kitchen. When time is of the essence, we find ourselves using ready washed salad leaves, ready-chopped tomatoes in concentrated tomato juice, ready-rolled puff and filo pastry, even on occasion, ready-to-use fresh garlic and ginger purées.

We have frequently dipped into this cornucopia of good things when composing the recipes you will find in this book. The hundred or so dishes may not answer the age-old question 'What on earth can I make for dinner on Wednesday night?', but we hope they will help to balance that difficult equation which has on one side the wish to entertain friends, on the other the demands of work and family.

All the recipes come with a first-class pedigree that combines pleasure in preparing and eating with wonderful taste, texture and colour. They've all been developed by us in our test kitchen, then fine-tuned after each Master Class to ensure that the instructions are crystal-clear to even the novice cook.

Bon appetit!

Evelyn Rose
Sula Leon

A Few of Our Favourite Things

To prepare our kind of food within a reasonable time scale – and to get the maximum pleasure on the way – you do need to have to hand a small but carefully chosen 'batterie de cuisine'. You can of course turn out superb dishes with little more than a few sharp knives and a chopping board – the chefs who developed the French classic cuisine did so with nothing more, give or take a sieve or three. But they did have a large and cheap supply of kitchen hands to do the donkey work for them. For the single-handed cook of today the knives are still as essential as ever, but they do need to be backed up with some of the products of modern kitchen technology. There's nothing like a food processor, for example, for taking the labour out of cooking and leaving you with all the fun.

FOOD PROCESSOR
Indispensable for all labour-intensive jobs such as chopping, puréeing and pastry-making. You can also make a creditable cake with one. It's good policy to buy a size a little larger than you think you'll need – state-of-the-art models can handle small as well as large quantities with equal efficiency.

BLENDER
Produces the smoothest soups and sauces – the goblet should have at least a 1 litre (1¾ pint) capacity.

MICROWAVE
Not essential but a wonderful time-saver for jobs such as melting chocolate and butter, reheating pasta, rice and other grains, making sauces and reheating vegetables with minimum loss of colour and vitamins. Also cooks fish to perfection.

PLAIN ROLLING PIN (WITHOUT HANDLES)
MADE FROM A HARD WOOD SUCH AS BEECH
In addition to rolling out pastry with the greatest degree of control, it's useful for crushing small quantities of bread and biscuit crumbs, for example, and also doubling as a pestle for crushing whole spices.

2-IN-I ZESTER/CANELLE KNIFE
With the zester, small quantities of grated zest can be removed from citrus fruit – a quick rinse under the tap is the only cleaning required. With the canelle part, those so inclined can score lemons, cucumbers or courgettes to make decorative slices.

ASSORTED BAKING TRAYS
(DIFFERENT SIZES AND DEPTHS)

For all kinds of baking and roasting. A good investment are ones made from pressed aluminium: this does not buckle or distort in the heat of the oven and can be cleaned with the very minimum of effort.

ASSORTED LOOSE-BOTTOMED METAL TART TINS

For sweet tartes choose rectangular, square or oblong shapes for variety; for savoury ones round tins should be 1–1½ inches (2.5–3.75 cm) deep so that there is a generous ratio of filling to pastry.

HAND-HELD ELECTRIC WHISK

In an ideal world a balloon whisk would be used as it undoubtedly produces the largest volume, of meringue, for instance. However occasional cooks don't do this job often enough to develop the necessary arm-power; we prefer to let the electric whisk take the strain out of this job as well as others such as whisking potatoes to creamy perfection at the stove.

FUEL AND HEATING-EFFICIENT PANS

A few sources of heat such as the induction and the halogen hob do demand pans made of specific materials – and manufacturers' recommendations should always be followed. However, whatever the heat source, pans that are to be efficient do need to sit level on the cooker and have well-fitting lids, as well as handles and knobs that are cool to handle. Besides regular saucepans for all kinds of cooking where liquids are involved, we find a (9½–11 inch/24–28 cm) lidded sauté pan is versatile for both frying and braising, while a 7 inch (17.5 cm) heavy-based crêpe pan (preferably with a top-quality non-stick interior) is useful for sautéeing small quantities of spices, garlic and fresh ginger, as well as dry-frying nuts to develop both colour and flavour.

RELIABLE AND EFFICIENT SCALES

The most accurate and time-efficient although the most expensive are the digital electronic kind. However, any scale worthy of its place in the batterie de cuisine should be designed to weigh ingredients in any shape container and then if necessary be reset to zero for weighing any additions. It should also be capable of weighing in both metric and imperial amounts by ½ oz and 10 g amounts up to 5 lb (2.25 kg).

RUBBER SPATULA

Indispensable for 'scraping down' the food processor bowl to ensure even processing and for removing every trace of mixture from any kind of bowl. It's also our favourite tool for mixing delicate mixtures such as mousses, creams and meringues with the minimum loss of air.

A Quartet of Knives

1)   A cook's knife (8 inch/20 cm blade). An all-purpose knife for chopping and slicing.

2)   A smaller cook's knife (6–7 inch/15–17.5 cm) blade). For smaller amounts of food.

3)   A serrated-edge knife with a round 4 inch (10 cm) blade. For slicing fruits and vegetables such as cucumber, tomatoes, citrus fruits and berries.

4)   A knife with a 3 inch (7.5 cm) pointed blade. For any job requiring a narrow 'incision' e.g. for testing the done-ness of vegetables and fruits.

Knife Sharpener
The pull-through variety with milled-steel rollers is both efficient and easy to use.

Swivel-blade Potato Peeler
Removes a thin peeling with the greatest ease from root vegetables and fruit.

How to Use the Recipes

S O L I D   A N D   L I Q U I D   M E A S U R E S

Solid measures are first given in spoons, pounds and ounces. Liquid measures are first given in spoons, pints or fluid ounces. Within the brackets that follow these measures, the first figure given is the metric equivalent and the second is the American equivalent measure in cups: e.g.

3 oz (75 g/⅓ cup) – solid measure
5 fl oz (150 ml/⅔ cup) – liquid measure

T E M P E R A T U R E S

These are first expressed as a gas number and then in degrees: e.g.

Gas 3 (325°F, 160°C)

L E N G T H   M E A S U R E M E N T S

These are first given in inches and then in centimetres: e.g.

2 inches (5 cm)

S P O O N   M E A S U R E S

These are level. As we find the use of millilitres to express spoon capacity unnecessarily complicated, we have used household (imperial measure) tablespoons and teaspoons throughout. (The tablespoon has a capacity of 15 ml, the teaspoon 5 ml.) As the difference in volume is so small we have assumed British and American spoons to be interchangeable, but some adjustment in the quantity of seasonings may be necessary to suit individual tastes.

B U T T E R

This is lightly salted, unless unsalted is specified.

M A R G A R I N E

Use a soft variety labelled 'high in polyunsaturates', unless a block of firm margarine is specified.

S U G A R

Normally this is granulated unless caster (superfine), icing (confectioner's) or a variety of brown sugar is specified. There is no standardised nomenclature for brown sugar but provided some kind of soft light- or medium-brown sugar (*not* the granular demerara sugar unless specified) is used, the exact shade of brown is not important. However, unless specified, the very dark-brown .molasses sugar should *not* be used as its treacly flavour and colour can overwhelm the other ingredients in a dish.

E G G S

These are size 3 – approximately 2½ oz (60–65 g) in weight. The egg size is only critical when 4 or more eggs are used in a recipe; in that case extra large (or small) eggs can upset the ratio of liquids to solids.

F L O U R

This is plain unless self-raising is specified. American readers should use 'cake' flour plus baking powder:
4 oz (125 g/1 cup) plain flour + 1 level teaspoon baking powder = 4 oz (125 g/ 1 cup) self-raising flour.

T I N   A N D   P A N   S I Z E S

These are given for guidance only, and those of approximately the same size can be used, provided they are the same depth or deeper than specified.

O V E N   T E M P E R A T U R E S

These are given for guidance only, as different ovens vary in the distribution of heat and the time taken to complete the cooking of a particular food. This is most marked when a fan-assisted or forced-air oven is used, and here you should follow the manufacturers' instructions for cooking something similar.

Glossary of British and American Terms

We give here the US equivalents of British foods and cooking terms.

UK	US
plain flour	all-purpose flour
supreme sponge self-raising flour	cake flour plus baking powder
wholemeal flour	wholewheat flour
granary flour	wholewheat flour with malted grains
cornflour	cornstarch
caster sugar	superfine sugar
icing sugar	confectioners' sugar
light Muscovado sugar	soft brown sugar
medium Muscovado sugar	soft brown sugar
golden syrup	corn syrup
bicarbonate of soda	baking soda
hazelnuts	filberts
pine kernels	pine nuts
glacé cherries	candied cherries
glacé pineapple	candied pineapple
drinking chocolate	instant chocolate
plain chocolate	semi-sweet chocolate
white fat	vegetable shortening
vanilla essence	vanilla extract
single cream	light cream
whipping or double cream	heavy cream
aubergines	eggplants
courgettes	zucchini
mangetout	snow peas
petit pois	spring peas
spring onions	green onions/scallions
Galia, Ogen or Charentais melons	musk melon or cantaloupe
Morello cherries	sour red cherries
haricot beans	navy beans
savoury biscuits	crackers
digestive biscuits	graham crackers
biscuits	cookies
minced meat (beef, veal or lamb)	ground meat (beef, veal or lamb)
to grill	to broil
the grill	the broiler

The First Course

Eye-catching and appetite-teasing, starters should never completely satisfy, rather act as a curtain raiser to the meal ahead.

Whether you choose an hors d'oeuvre, a richly flavoured soup, or a salad Californian style depends on the balance of the menu, the season and the amount of time you are prepared to invest in this course.

The home cook can especially delight with a bowl of soup – a dish considered too lowly for many restaurants, yet so easy to prepare (a good commercial stock is the name of the game). Soups are ideal for preparing ahead as they conveniently improve in flavour when made a day or two in advance and stored in the fridge, and most freeze well, too.

When it comes to hors d'oeuvres – whether fish or meat, vegetable or pastry – we don't attempt to compete with the professional presentations of the chef. If all the components are ready in advance, happily chilling and crisping in the fridge, they can be given sparkle simply by arranging on individual glass plates just before serving, adding a tiny bouquet of unusual salad leaves or a few artfully arranged sprigs of a decorative herb such as lacy-leaved chervil or tarragon.

SOUPS

Creamy Watercress and Walnut Soup

SERVES 6–8

Keeps 2 days under refrigeration. Freeze the pureé 2 months

A cream soup, but with a tang – the perfect starter before a main course of plainly grilled fish. Use walnut halves – the cheaper walnut pieces are often dusty, coming from the bottom of the sack.

3 packs (9 oz/250 g) watercress

1½ oz (40 g/3 tbsp) butter

1 medium onion (5 oz/150 g), finely chopped

the white part of a fat leek, finely sliced

8 oz (225 g) potatoes, peeled and thinly sliced

2 pints (1.1 litre/5 cups) hot water with 3 vegetable stock cubes

1 bay leaf

1½ teasp salt

15 grinds black pepper

10 fl oz (275 ml/1¼ cups) milk

4 oz (125 g/1 cup) walnut halves (reserve 2 tbsp for garnish)

5 fl oz (150 ml/⅔ cup) crème fraîche (reserve 2 tbsp for garnish)

2 tbsp walnut oil

1 Wash and spin dry all the watercress. Cut off 6 or 8 sprigs from one of the bunches and reserve. Chop the remainder, re-wrap and refrigerate.

2 Melt the butter in a soup pan, add the onion and leek and sauté, covered, for 5 minutes until soft and golden.

3 Add the potatoes, stock, bay leaf and seasonings, bring to the boil, cover and simmer for 20 minutes until the potatoes are tender.

4 Add the majority of the remaining watercress, stalks as well as leaves (reserve some for later). Bring back to the boil and simmer, *uncovered*, for 2 minutes. This preserves the colour.

5 Pureé in a blender or food processor until absolutely smooth. Return the purée to the rinsed pan and bring slowly to simmering point, then stir in the milk. Remove from the heat and leave covered until cool. Refrigerate for at least 12 hours.

6 Meanwhile, toss the walnuts in a small heavy frying pan over medium heat until they smell 'toasty'. When cool, chop finely and reserve 2 tbsp for the garnish.

TO SERVE

Add the bulk of the walnuts to the soup and reheat until simmering, then stir in the reserved chopped watercress leaves, the crème fraîche (reserve 2 tbsp for garnish) and the nut oil. Taste and add extra salt if necessary. Garnish each serving with a little crème fraîche, a sprig of watercress and a scattering of walnuts.

Soupe au Pistou

SERVES 6–8

Keeps 2 days under refrigeration. Freeze 3 months

The Provençale answer to minestrone is fragrant with the first young basil of the Mediterranean spring. Instead of making your own pistou, you can use a small jar of ready-to-use pesto.

1 large (8 oz/225 g) onion, finely chopped

1 tbsp extra virgin olive oil

1 large (8 oz/225 g) potato, peeled and cut into ⅜ inch (1 cm) dice

1 fat stick celery, diced

the white and pale green part of a medium leek, finely sliced

3½ pints (2 litres/7½ cups) hot water with 4 vegetable stock cubes

20 grinds black pepper

8 oz (225 g) fresh or frozen green beans, cut into ½ inch (1.25 cm) lengths

1 × 8 oz (225 g) can haricot beans, drained

2 rounded tbsp tomato purée

1 oz (25 g) vermicelli, crushed to break up the lengths

FOR THE PISTOU
2 medium cloves garlic

1 handful (¾ oz/20 g) fresh basil leaves

4 tbsp extra virgin olive oil

2 tbsp hot liquid from soup

FOR THE GARNISH (OPTIONAL)
finely grated Parmesan cheese

1 In a large 4 pint/2.25 litre/10 cup) soup pan, gently sauté the onion in the oil, covering the pan, until golden.

2 Add the potato, celery and leek with the stock and pepper, cover and simmer for 15 minutes.

3 Now add the green beans, haricot beans and tomato purée and simmer for a further 10 minutes.

4 To make the pistou, process all the ingredients in the food processor until smooth and thick.

TO SERVE

Bring the soup to boiling point, add the vermicelli, then simmer for 3 minutes. Taste for seasoning. Spoon into soup cups and top with a small spoonful of the pistou. Serve plain or with the grated cheese.

Cream of Artichoke and Hazelnut Soup

S E R V E S   8

Keeps 3 days under refrigeration. Freeze 2 months

A gently flavoured soup for the nut lover. Poached or baked salmon would make a compatible dish to follow.

2 × 15 oz (425 g) cans artichoke bottoms or hearts

3½ oz (100 g/7 tbsp) butter

3 oz (75 g) shallots, finely chopped

15 fl oz (425 ml/2 cups) hot water with 1 vegetable stock cube

1¼ pints (725 ml/3 cups) milk

2 tbsp cornflour

18 grinds black pepper

1½ teasp salt

3 oz (75 g/¾ cup) ground hazelnuts (reserve 1 tbsp for garnish)

5 fl oz (150 ml/⅔ cup) single cream or 'half and half' milk and single cream

a few chervil leaves

1 Drain the artichoke bottoms, reserve two and slice the others. Put them in a small pan with 1½ oz (40 g/3 tbsp) of the butter, cover and cook very gently for 10 minutes without allowing them to brown.

2 In a large soup pan, cook the shallots gently in the remaining butter until golden, then add the hot stock and 1 pint (575 ml/2½ cups) of the milk. Mix the remaining milk smoothly with the cornflour and add to the pan with the seasonings. Bring to the boil and simmer for 4 minutes.

3 Add the bulk of the ground hazelnuts and sliced artichoke bottoms, and purée in the blender until absolutely smooth. Return to the pan and allow to stand for several hours.

T o   s e r v e

Cut the two remaining artichokes into little cubes, and add to the soup along with the cream. Reheat until steaming, and garnish with chervil leaves and the reserved ground hazelnuts.

Tuscan Tomato and Bean Soup with a Parsley Pesto Sauce

SERVES 6–8

Keeps 3 days under refrigeration. Freeze 3 months

The parsley pesto transforms this hearty country soup into one that is rich and rare. The only difficult thing about it is to remember to soak the beans in advance – but it's worth it!

8 oz (225 g/1¼ cups) dried cannellini or haricot beans

1½ tbsp extra virgin olive oil

1 medium onion (5 oz/150 g), finely chopped in the food processor

1 large carrot, coarsely chopped in the food processor

2 sticks celery, coarsely chopped in the food processor

2½ pints (1.4 litres/6¼ cups) hot water with 3 vegetable stock cubes

1 level tbsp tomato purée

1 teasp salt

15 grinds black pepper

½ teasp sugar

FOR THE PESTO SAUCE

1½ cups parsley leaves, loosely packed

3 cloves garlic

½ teasp salt, preferably coarse sea salt

4 tbsp extra virgin olive oil

6 tbsp grated Parmesan cheese

1 Soak the beans in cold water to cover overnight.

2 Heat the oil in a large soup pan and sauté the onion until golden, then add the carrot and celery and cook for a further 5 minutes, stirring occasionally. Add the stock, the tomato purée, salt, pepper and sugar and bring to the boil.

3 Drain the beans, rinse under the tap then add to the pot. Cover and simmer very slowly either on top of the stove or in the oven at Gas 2 (300°F, 150°C) until the beans are absolutely tender, about 1 hour.

4 Remove half the beans and a little of the soup and purée in a blender or food processor, then return to the pan. Leave for several hours.

5 To make the pesto sauce, put all the ingredients into the food processor and process until thick and even in texture.

TO SERVE

Reheat the soup, taste for seasoning, then garnish each bowl with a generous spoonful of sauce.

Red Lentil Soup with Fresh Ginger and Spiced Oil

SERVES 6–8

Keeps 3 days under refrigeration. Freeze 2 months (but spices may fade)

The humble lentil is given an entirely new image in this lightly spiced soup. The spiced oil packs a pleasing punch.

10 oz (275 g/1½ cups) red lentils

12 oz (350 g) onions, finely chopped

3 large cloves garlic, chopped

3 tbsp extra virgin olive oil

1½ tbsp peeled and coarsely chopped fresh ginger

1½ teasp ground cumin

1½ teasp coriander seeds

3 pints (1.75 litres/7½ cups) hot water with 4 vegetable or chicken stock cubes

1 × 14 oz (140 g) can chopped tomatoes in concentrated juice

1 teasp fine sea salt

15 grinds black pepper

2 teasp granulated sugar

FOR THE SPICED OIL
3 tbsp sunflower oil

1 pinch dried hot red pepper flakes

½ teasp cumin seeds

1 good pinch ground turmeric

FOR THE GARNISH
sprigs of fresh coriander or parsley

mini poppadoms

1 Cover the lentils with boiling water for 15 minutes, then rinse in cold water and drain.

2 In a large soup pan, sauté the onion and garlic in the olive oil over moderate heat until softened and golden (keep the lid on).

3 Add the ginger and cook for a minute, then add the ground cumin and coriander seeds and cook for a further minute.

4 Add the lentils, stock, tomatoes, salt, pepper and sugar and simmer, covered, for 20 minutes or until the lentils are tender.

5 Cool until it stops steaming, then purée in a blender or food processor. Return to the cleaned pan and leave for several hours or for up to 3 days in the refrigerator.

6 To make the spiced oil, in a small crêpe or frying pan, heat the sunflower oil until you can feel a comfortable heat on your hand held 2 inches (5 cm) above it. Add the pepper flakes, cumin seeds and turmeric and fry for 10 seconds only, to release the flavours, then remove from the heat.

TO SERVE

Reheat the soup and ladle it into individual bowls. Drizzle a teaspoon of the spiced oil over each serving and garnish with a sprig of herb. Serve with the poppadoms.

Butternut Squash Soup with Ginger and Lime

SERVES 6–8

Keeps 3 days under refrigeration. Freeze 2 months

A cousin of the pumpkin (which can be used as a substitute) and relatively new to supermarket shelves, this banana-coloured squash makes a beautiful golden soup light enough to serve before roast or grilled meat or poultry.

1 medium onion (5 oz/150 g), finely chopped

1½ tbsp peeled and coarsely chopped fresh ginger

2 fat cloves garlic, chopped

2 oz (50 g/4 tbsp) butter or margarine

2 lb (900 g) butternut squash, peeled, seeded and thinly sliced

2 pints (1.1 litre/5 cups) hot water with 3 chicken or vegetable stock cubes

2 teasp fresh lime juice

15 grinds black pepper

½ teasp salt

FOR THE GARNISH
3 tbsp thin strips of peeled fresh ginger

2 tbsp sunflower oil

3 teasp thin strips of lime peel (from 1 lime)

2 tbsp toasted pine kernels

1 In a large soup pan, sauté the onion, ginger and garlic in the fat, covered, until the onion is soft and golden.

2 Add the squash and stock, bring to the boil then simmer, covered, for 20 minutes or until the squash feels absolutely tender when pierced with a slim sharp knife.

3 Purée in a blender or food processor until completely smooth, then return to the pan. Stir in the lime juice, pepper and salt. Taste for seasoning then reheat until barely bubbling. The soup can be refrigerated for up to 3 days at this point.

4 For the garnish, sauté the ginger strips in the oil until a pale gold then drain on crumpled paper.

TO SERVE

Divide the soup between bowls, and garnish with the fried ginger and the lime rind and pine kernels.

Aubergine and Coriander Soup with a Red Pepper and Cream Garnish

SERVES 6–8

Soup and garnish keep 3 days under refrigeration. Soup freezes 3 months

Very pretty as well as richly flavoured, the scarlet pepper garnish contrasting with the deep-coloured soup.

3 tbsp extra virgin olive oil

1½ lb (675 g) aubergines, peeled and chopped

1 medium onion (5 oz/150 g), finely chopped

2 medium cloves garlic, chopped

3 pints (1.75 litres/7½ cups) hot water with 4 vegetable stock cubes

1 teasp ground coriander

1 teasp salt

20 grinds black pepper

3 tbsp Amontillado sherry

FOR THE GARNISH
2 large canned red peppers, drained, dried and roughly chopped

4 tbsp single cream or crème fraîche

½ teasp salt

½ teasp mild chilli powder

15 grinds black pepper

1 Heat the oil in a soup pan and sauté the aubergines, onion and garlic, covered, for 20 minutes or until golden and tender.

2 Purée in a blender with the stock, coriander, salt and pepper until smooth.

3 Return to the rinsed pan, bring to the boil, re-season with extra salt and pepper if necessary, then allow to stand for several hours.

4 For the garnish, purée the chopped red pepper and the cream in the blender with the seasonings until absolutely smooth. Refrigerate until serving time.

TO SERVE

Reheat the soup with the sherry and serve with some of the pepper garnish swirled on top.

Sweet and Sour Tomato and Vermicelli Soup

SERVES 6–8

Keeps 3 days under refrigeration. Freezes 3 months

The deep rich flavour of this soup belies the speed and simplicity of its preparation. Rice noodles give it a particularly interesting texture.

3 pints (1.75 litres/7½ cups) hot strong chicken stock (home-made or using 4 cubes)

1 × 14 oz (140 g) can finely chopped tomatoes in concentrated tomato juice

3 tbsp lemon juice

½ teasp salt

15 grinds black pepper

2 tbsp light Muscovado (brown) sugar

2 level tbsp tomato purée

a handful of vermicelli (about 2 oz/50 g) or rice noodles, crushed to break up the lengths

I Put all the ingredients (except the vermicelli) into a large soup pan. Bring to the boil, cover and simmer for 25 minutes.

2 Add the vermicelli and continue to simmer for a further 5 minutes. Taste and add more lemon juice and/or sugar if desired.

TO SERVE

If possible, leave for several hours or overnight to mature. However it still tastes delicious if served immediately.

Hungarian Cherry Soup

S E R V E S   6 – 8

Keeps 3 days under refrigeration. Freeze 2 months

You don't have to go to Budapest – cans of excellent Morello cherries now imported from Eastern Europe make this beautiful pale pink soup easy to prepare in the West. And the flavour is quite memorable. If pitted cherries are not available, don't try to remove the stones – just warn your guests!

1 × 1½ lb (675 g) jar pitted Morello cherries in syrup

juice strained from cherries (should be 12 fl oz/350 ml/1½ cups)

7 fl oz (200 ml/¾ cup + 2 tbsp) port-type wine

1½ pints (850 ml/3¾ cups) water

2 oz (50g/¼ cup) sugar

grated rind of ½ lemon

½ teasp salt

1 cinnamon stick

1 tbsp cornflour mixed to a cream with 1 teasp lemon juice and 1 tbsp water

10 fl oz (275 ml/1¼ cups) soured cream

1 Put the strained juice, wine, water, sugar, lemon rind, salt and cinnamon stick into a soup pan, bring to the boil and bubble uncovered for 7 minutes.

2 Add the cherries and the cornflour liquid, bring back to the boil and simmer for 3 minutes until clear.

3 Cool until it stops steaming, then refrigerate until it is absolutely cold.

4 Put the soured cream in a bowl and add a ladle or two of the cold cherry mixture, whisking until smooth. Pour this creamy liquid back into the cherry mixture and chill until just before serving.

T O   S E R V E

Serve cold but not icy.

Calamata Olive and Sun-Dried Tomato Loaf

MAKES 1 LOAF

The well-wrapped bread keeps 1 week in the refrigerator, 1 month in the freezer

This makes a really original yeast-free bread to serve with soups and salads. To make life easy, buy these ready-to-serve and concentrate your efforts on this fun loaf.

6 oz (175 g/1½ cups) plain flour

1 teasp baking powder

½ teasp bicarbonate of soda

½ teasp salt

2 teasp caster sugar

3 level tbsp drained and chopped sun-dried tomatoes in oil (reserve 1 tbsp oil)

1 clove garlic, chopped

½ teasp freeze-dried rosemary, or 2 teasp fresh, finely chopped

15 grinds black pepper

1 egg

5 fl oz (150 ml/⅔ cup) milk

1 tbsp + 1 teasp sunflower oil

2 oz (50 g/½ cup) Calamata or other black olives, stoned and chopped

1 tbsp drained capers, finely chopped

3 tbsp finely chopped parsley

1 oz (25 g/¼ cup) finely grated Parmesan or other sharp cheese

Preheat the oven to Gas 4 (350°F, 180°C).

1 Grease a 1 lb (450 g) loaf tin and line the bottom with a strip of silicone paper.

2 In a bowl mix the flour, baking powder, bicarbonate of soda, salt and sugar.

3 In a small frying pan heat the oil reserved from the sun-dried tomatoes. Cook the garlic in this over a moderate heat with the rosemary and black pepper until pale gold and fragrant but not brown.

4 In a large bowl whisk together the egg, the milk, the sunflower oil and the garlic mixture. Add the dry ingredients and stir until combined. Stir in the tomatoes, olives, capers, parsley and Parmesan.

5 Spoon into the prepared tin and bake for 35–40 minutes or until a skewer comes out clean. Remove the loaf from the tin and leave to cool, right side up, on a rack.

TO SERVE

Serve sliced, and buttered if desired.

Goat's Cheese and Sun-Dried Tomato Toasts

SERVES 6–8

Serve freshly made, though toast can be made in advance

These versatile mouthfuls can be served with drinks to pep up a ready-to-serve soup, or as a light starter with a salad of mixed leaves.

1 × 14 inch (35 cm) (approx.) brown or white baguette

2 rounded tbsp creamy fromage frais or Greek yoghurt

5 oz (150 g) mild goat's cheese

2 tbsp mixed fresh herbs, finely chopped (e.g. parsley, chives, oregano)

6 tbsp (approx.) extra virgin olive oil

4 sun-dried tomatoes, drained (or 1 can anchovies, drained), cut in thin strips

freshly ground black pepper

Preheat the oven to Gas 7 (425°F, 220°C), or turn on the grill.

1 Cut the bread into about sixteen slanting slices, each ⅜ inch (1 cm) thick.

2 Add enough of the fromage frais to the cheese to make a creamy spread then stir in half the chopped herbs and set aside.

3 Brush one side of the bread with olive oil and bake or grill until a light gold in colour. Turn and brown the unoiled side.

4 Spread a thick layer of cheese over the oiled side of the bread and arrange the sun-dried tomato or anchovy strips decoratively on top. (The toasts may be left ready to cook at this stage.)

5 Bake or grill the toasts until the cheese is lightly coloured, about 3 minutes.

TO SERVE

Sprinkle with the remaining herbs and a grinding of black pepper.

STARTERS

Creamy Blue Cheese Tartelettes from La Bresse

MAKES EIGHT 3–4 INCH (7.5–10 CM) TARTELETTES

Uncooked and baked pastry keeps 2 days under refrigeration. Freeze 3 months. Baked cases can be filled and then frozen uncooked. They do not need to be thawed before cooking, but allow 5 minutes longer in the oven

These make an elegant main course for a vegetarian luncheon or a starter before a salad main course. The filling is particularly unctuous in texture.

1 recipe Brown Herb Pastry (see page 125)

FOR THE FILLING
5 oz (150 g/⅔ cup) cream cheese

3 oz (75 g/⅓ cup) Bleu de Bresse or other blue cheese, crumbled

1 oz (25 g/2 tbsp) butter

3 eggs, lightly beaten

12 fl oz (350 ml/1½ cups) double cream or crème fraîche

15 grinds black pepper

1 tbsp finely snipped chives

a little salt

1 Roll out the pastry to fit the tartelette cases. Prick all over with a fork then press a piece of foil into each tartelette case, moulding it into shape.

2 Freeze for 30 minutes then bake at Gas 7 (425°F, 220°C) for 5–7 minutes until the pastry is set and firm to the touch. Remove the foil, prick the base again and continue to bake for a further 5–7 minutes until quite dry to the touch and only lightly coloured. Set to one side.

3 To make the filling, cream the two cheeses and the butter together in a bowl then add the beaten eggs followed by the cream or crème fraîche, pepper and chives. Taste and add a little salt if necessary.

4 Divide the filling between the tartelettes, filling them to the brim. Bake at Gas 6 (400°F, 200°C) for 20 minutes or until golden.

TO SERVE
Serve at room temperature with a Spring Garland Salad (see page 27).

Ginger-Spiked Chicken-Liver Pâté on Crostini

SERVES 6–8 PLUS LEFTOVERS, OR 10–12 AS A SPREAD

Pâté keeps 5 days under refrigeration. Freeze 1 month

A smooth, delicately flavoured pâté, with the ginger adding an unexpected zing! The pâté is best prepared at least a day in advance to allow the flavours to develop.

4 eggs

1 large onion (8 oz/225 g), finely chopped

3 oz (75 g/⅓ cup) butter, or 5 level tbsp rendered chicken fat

1 large clove garlic, finely chopped

2 tbsp finely chopped peeled ginger

1 teasp sea salt

20 grinds black pepper

¼ teasp ground nutmeg

1 lb (450 g) chicken livers, grilled or sautéed (see below)

3 tbsp brandy

FOR THE CROSTINI
1 French stick, cut in ⅜ inch (1 cm) thick slices

extra virgin olive oil

2 rounded tbsp slivers peeled ginger

a little sunflower oil

1 Boil the eggs for 10 minutes then drench with cold water and leave.

2 Sauté the onion in the fat until beginning to caramelise then add the garlic and ginger and continue to cook for a further 2–3 minutes until an aroma arises.

3 Sprinkle with the seasonings then add the halved sautéed or grilled livers (cooked through but not crisp), and toss gently to absorb the flavours in the pan. (If preferred, the raw livers can be halved and sautéed at this stage, until just cooked through.) Pour the brandy into the pan and allow to bubble until it has almost evaporated.

4 Turn into the food processor together with the shelled and halved hard-boiled eggs and process until absolutely smooth, cleaning down the sides of the bowl as necessary. Turn into a bowl, cover and leave refrigerated for several hours for the flavours to develop. An hour before using, leave at room temperature.

5 To make the crostini, brush one side of each slice of bread with olive oil, grill until golden brown then turn and toast the un-oiled side. These can now be left for several hours.

6 Meanwhile fry the slivers of ginger in a little hot sunflower oil, drain on paper towels then set aside.

Spread each crostini generously (on the oiled side) with pâté (use a piping bag or a fork), and spike with the ginger slivers. Serve as a starter or with drinks.

Alternatively the pâté can be divided between little pots and the surface of each spiked with the ginger slivers. Serve with toasted brioche.

A Pâté of Chicken Livers and Pistachios with a Port and Redcurrant Sauce

SERVES 6–8

Pâté keeps 5 days under refrigeration, sauce 2 weeks. Pâté freezes 1 month, sauce 3 months

A very pretty and particularly flavourful combination. The sauce echoes the sweetness of the pâté.

1 quantity Chicken Liver Pâté (see page 14), omitting the ginger

2 oz (50 g/½ cup) natural shelled pistachios, finely chopped

15 g (½ oz) fresh tarragon, finely chopped

FOR THE SAUCE
8 oz (225 g) redcurrant jelly

juice of 1 orange and 1 lemon (5 fl oz/150 ml/⅔ cup altogether)

2 level teasp cornflour

4 tbsp port or port-type wine

Prepare both the pâté and the sauce 24 hours in advance and refrigerate.

1 To make the sauce, put the redcurrant jelly into a small pan, add the citrus juices and bring slowly to the boil, whisking gently until the jelly has melted down. Mix the cornflour smoothly with the port then add to the pan and bubble for 3 minutes until the mixture looks clear. Pour into a jug with a narrow spout and chill.

2 Next day shape the pâté mixture by laying it on clingfilm and moulding it into a cylinder about 2 inches (5 cm) in diameter and 12 inches (30 cm) long. Chill again until firm.

3 To coat the pâté, sprinkle the nuts and tarragon evenly on a piece of foil. Carefully unwrap the pâté then roll it evenly in the nut/tarragon mixture. It can now be covered with the foil and chilled again, or cut at once into ¾ inch (2 cm) thick diagonal slices.

TO SERVE
Arrange two slices per serving on glass or other small plates. Pour a little pool of the sauce at the side. Serve with freshly baked ciabatta bread.

Pecan and Smoked Salmon Roulade with a Jewelled Salad

SERVES 6–8

Salmon pâté keeps 3 days under refrigeration. The complete dish keeps 2 days. Freeze pâté only 1 month

A piquant starter for a summer meal that needs the minimum of last-minute preparation.

8 oz (225 g) best smoked salmon	**FOR THE SALAD**
4 oz (125 g/½ cup) ricotta or cream cheese	2 large tomatoes
1–2 tbsp lemon juice	1 small red pepper
1 tbsp creamed horseradish	1 small yellow pepper
10 grinds black pepper	½ large cucumber
1 tbsp fresh snipped dill	coarse salt
2 oz (50 g/½ cup) shelled pecan nuts, toasted then finely chopped	5 tbsp Master Class Vinaigrette (see page 32)
2 tbsp finely chopped parsley	2 teasp redcurrant jelly
	1 small pack mixed salad leaves

Prepare and refrigerate the roulade the day before.

1 Work the smoked salmon in the food processor with the ricotta or cream cheese, the lemon juice, horseradish, black pepper and dill until absolutely smooth. Taste for seasoning.

2 Shape the pâté mixture by laying it on clingfilm then rolling and moulding it into a cylinder about 2 inches (5 cm) in diameter and 10 inches (25 cm) long.

3 To prepare the salad, cut each of the vegetables into ⅜ inch (1 cm) cubes. Put the cucumber in a salad spinner, sprinkle with coarse salt and leave for 30 minutes. Rinse then spin dry. Mix with the tomato and peppers and then with the dressing and jelly. Chill.

4 Sprinkle the finely chopped pecan nuts and parsley on a sheet of foil covered with clingfilm. Carefully remove the original clingfilm then roll the roulade evenly in the nut and parsley mixture. Cover with the fresh clingfilm and foil and chill until required.

TO SERVE

Cut in six to eight diagonal slices and arrange on a small bed of the salad leaves topped with the jewelled salad. Serve with Melba toast or slices of buttered French bread.

Grilled Aubergines Topped with a Piquant Mixed Pepper Salad

S E R V E S   6 – 8   A S   A   S T A R T E R

The salad keeps 2 days under refrigeration

Preparing the pepper salad the day before is not only convenient but allows the glorious flavours to develop fully. Instead of the six fresh peppers, you can use a 15 oz (425 g) can grilled red peppers in brine plus two fresh yellow peppers, grilled as below. The aubergines can be grilled at the same time or freshly on the day.

2 × ¾–1 lb (350–450 g) aubergines, cut in diagonal slices ⅜ inch (1 cm) thick

extra virgin olive oil

FOR THE PEPPER SALAD
4 fresh red and 2 yellow peppers, halved then pith and seeds removed

1 oz (25 g) fresh basil leaves, chopped

4 fl oz (125 ml/½ cup) extra virgin olive oil

4 large garlic cloves, crushed

3 tbsp balsamic or sherry vinegar

1 rounded tbsp currants

FOR THE GARNISH
18–24 fat black olives

1½ oz (40g/⅓ cup) toasted pine kernels

1 Brush both sides of the aubergine slices and the skin side of the fresh peppers with extra virgin olive oil, then arrange the vegetables in an oiled grill pan. Grill until the aubergines are golden on both sides (turn once), and the skin of the peppers has blackened and feels papery all over – 10–15 minutes.

2 Cover the grilled peppers immediately with paper towels to soften the skin. Leave for 10 minutes when the skin can easily be stripped off. (If canned pimentos are used, drain well on paper towels.) The aubergine slices can now be piled into a shallow dish, covered and refrigerated.

3 Cut all the peppers into ½ inch (1.25 cm) strips.

4 In a medium bowl combine the chopped basil, the measured extra virgin olive oil, peppers, garlic, vinegar and currants and allow to stand, covered and chilled for at least 2 hours or overnight.

T O   S E R V E

Either on one large platter or individual plates, top the aubergines with the pepper salad, the olives and pine kernels and serve with a nut bread or warm brown rolls.

Mushrooms in White Wine, Turkish Style

SERVES 6–8

Keeps 4 days under refrigeration

A fruity more gently flavoured variation of the Greek dish, sweetened with some of the dried fruits for which Turkey is so famous.

2 lb (900 g/10 cups) button mushrooms

4 tbsp sultanas

1 large unpeeled lemon, thinly sliced and halved

2 rounded teasp tomato purée

1 × 3 oz (75 g) bunch spring onions, finely sliced

5 fl oz (150 ml/⅔ cup) dry white wine

1 teasp ground coriander

½ teasp garlic purée

3 tbsp extra virgin olive oil

1 pinch cayenne pepper

1 teasp salt

¼ teasp ground white pepper

1 large sprig parsley

1 bay leaf

FOR THE GARNISH
6–8 tiny sprigs thyme

1 Wipe the mushrooms with a damp cloth and cut the stalks level with the caps (keep the stalks for another use).

2 Put all the ingredients (except the mushrooms, sultanas and lemon slices) in a pan and mix well. Cover and bring to the boil, then simmer for 5 minutes.

3 Uncover, and add the mushrooms, sultanas and lemon slices. Spoon the liquid over, then cover and simmer for 8–10 minutes or until the mushrooms are just tender. Turn into a bowl and chill for several hours. Remove the herbs.

TO SERVE

Divide between small cocottes and garnish with a sprig of fresh thyme. Serve with warm brown rolls or buttered brown French bread.

OPPOSITE, CLOCKWISE FROM TOP

Butternut Squash Soup with Ginger and Lime (page 7), *Creamy Watercress and Walnut Soup* (page 2), *A Calamata Olive and Sun-dried Tomato Loaf* (page 11), *Soup au Pistou* (page 3)

FACING PAGE 19, TOP TO BOTTOM

Grilled Aubergines Topped with a Piquant Mixed Pepper Salad (page 17), *A Pâté of Chicken Livers and Pistachios with a Port and Redcurrent Sauce* (page 15)

Asparagus Mimosa

SERVES 6–8

Serve the same day

This is an ideal way to serve thinner stalks of fresh asparagus or the miniature ones available out of season. The dressing has a high ratio of oil to vinegar so that it does not overwhelm but in fact enhances the delicate flavour of the vegetable. Ready-rolled pastry is a great time saver for this particular dish.

2 × 14 oz (140 g) packs puff pastry

1 egg yolk + 2 teasp cold water to glaze

2–3 × 3½ oz (100 g) packs fresh asparagus tips

salt

FOR THE DRESSING
3 tbsp hazelnut oil

6 tbsp extra virgin olive oil

¼ teasp salt

10 grinds black pepper

½ teasp dry mustard

1 good pinch caster sugar

1 tbsp snipped chives

1½ tbsp white wine or cider vinegar

FOR THE GARNISH
1 egg, hard-boiled and grated

3 tbsp toasted flaked or chopped hazelnuts

I Several hours in advance, put all the dressing ingredients into a screw-top jar and shake until thickened – 1–2 minutes.

Preheat the oven to Gas 8 (450°F, 230°C).

2 Cut the pastry into six to eight rectangles, each measuring 5 × 3 inches (12.5–7.5 cm). Roll with a lattice cutter, if available, and spread gently to show the pattern. Otherwise leave plain. Brush with the egg and water glaze and bake for 8 minutes or until a rich brown. Set aside.

3 To cook the asparagus, put in a lidded frying pan with boiling salted water to cover, and bring back to the boil. Cover and simmer 5–6 minutes until barely tender. Drain, drench with cold water to set the colour, drain again, then leave on paper towels to absorb any moisture.

TO SERVE

Just before dinner, assemble as follows: lay a rectangle of pastry on each plate, divide the asparagus tips between them (about 5 to a serving), spoon over a generous tbsp of the dressing and top with the mixed grated egg and hazelnuts. Serve with brown bread and butter.

A Roasted Vegetable and Goat's Cheese Terrine with Salsa Verde

SERVES 6–8

The terrine may be made 2 days in advance and kept under refrigeration. Do not freeze

The layers of aubergine, scarlet and cream, standing in a pool of green herb sauce, make a starter pretty enough to double as a table decoration.

2 lb (900 g) aubergines, cut lengthways into ½ inch (1.25 cm) thick slices

olive oil

salt

3 large red peppers

3 rounded tbsp of bought olive purée or tapenade

7 oz (200 g/1 cup) mild goat's cheese, Camembert or Vignotte, sliced

FOR THE SALSA VERDE
3 oz (75 g/approx. 1 cup) chopped mixed herbs (e.g. parsley, basil, dill, reserve a little for the garnish)

2 cloves garlic

1 oz (25 g/¼ cup) shelled walnuts

6 fl oz (175 ml/¾ cup) extra virgin olive oil

3 tbsp red wine vinegar

½ teasp salt

FOR THE GARNISH
tiny bouquets of the herbs

Preheat the grill.

1 Arrange the aubergine slices in one layer on baking sheets. Brush both sides with the oil, sprinkle lightly with salt and grill about 4 inches (10 cm) from the heat for 4–5 minutes on each side, or until golden and tender. Transfer to paper towels to drain.

2 Halve the red peppers, remove the pith and seeds, brush with olive oil and grill until the skin looks charred and papery. Remove and cover with paper towels for 5–10 minutes then lift off the skin and cut the peppers lengthways into three.

3 Line a dampened 1 lb (450 g) loaf tin with clingfilm, leaving a 3 inch (7.5 cm) overlap, and in it arrange the aubergine, olive paste, peppers and cheese in layers, beginning and ending with aubergine. You will thus have four layers of aubergine and three layers each of pepper strips, tapenade and goat's cheese.

4 Cover the top layer (aubergine) with the clingfilm overhang, weight the terrine down with 3 × 14 oz (140 g) cans and chill for 24 hours.

5 To make the salsa verde, put all the ingredients into the food processor and process until the walnuts and herbs are finely chopped. Pour into a container and chill.

TO SERVE
Remove the weights, invert the terrine on a cutting board and discard the clingfilm. Cut into ¾ inch (2 cm) thick slices with a well-sharpened knife. Pour enough of the

sauce to lightly cover each plate, tilting the plates to spread it evenly, and arrange a slice of the terrine on top. Garnish each serving with the herbs.

Bruschette with Artichoke Hearts and Mozzarella Cheese

SERVES 6–8

The bruschette can be prepared well in advance, but must be served straight from the oven

An appetiser to set the taste-buds tingling.

1 part-baked ciabatta loaf (olive or sun-dried tomato)

3 oz (75 g/⅓ cup) soft butter

2–3 cloves garlic, crushed

1 × 8–9 oz (225–250 g) jar artichokes in oil, drained and coarsely chopped

11 oz (300 g) Italian Mozzarella cheese, cut in thin slices

freshly ground black pepper

Preheat the oven to Gas 5 (375°F, 190°C).

1 Cut the bread into ten ¾ inch (2 cm) slices. Cream the butter and garlic together. Spread over the bread slices, cover with the chopped artichokes and top with the slices of cheese.

2 Arrange the slices side by side on baking trays and bake for 12–15 minutes until the cheese has melted and the edges are brown. Sprinkle with black pepper.

TO SERVE

Accompany with the Salad of Mixed Leaves, Physalis and Sharon Fruit (see page 30).

Individual Rösti with Smoked Salmon and Dilled Soured Cream

S E R V E S   6 – 8

Rösti keep for 2 days under refrigeration. Freeze for 3 months

With a mouth-watering blend of flavours, this is light and luscious – a perfect presentation for a summer luncheon. Ready-to-serve blinis may be used instead of the rösti.

12 oz (350 g) smoked salmon or gravlax, thinly sliced

a squeeze of lemon juice

freshly ground black pepper

8 fl oz (25 ml/1 cup) soured cream

1 × 15 g (½ oz) pack fresh dill, snipped (reserve a few fronds for garnish)

2 tbsp caviar (optional)

FOR THE RÖSTI

1½ lb (675 g) baking potatoes, peeled

½ medium onion

1 tbsp chopped fresh or frozen parsley

1 teasp salt

20 grinds black pepper

sunflower oil for shallow frying

1 Fifteen minutes before you are ready to cook the rösti, coarsely grate the potatoes and onion (as for grated cheese). Drain in a sieve, pressing down well to extract the starchy liquid.

2 Turn into a bowl and mix with the parsley and seasonings.

3 In a heavy frying pan, put enough oil to come to a depth of ½ inch (1.25 cm). When hot put in tablespoons of the mixture, flattening each rösti with the back of the spoon.

4 Cook over steady moderate heat for 3–4 minutes until the underside is a rich brown, then turn and cook the second side until brown. Drain on crumpled kitchen paper.

5 The freshly cooked rösti may be kept hot and crisp in the oven at Gas 3 (325°F, 160°C) for up to 15 minutes. Alternatively, they may be refrigerated overnight or frozen. To reheat, just before serving toss in a hot dry pan until heated through.

6 When ready to serve, season the salmon with the lemon juice and black pepper. Mix the soured cream and most of the dill.

TO SERVE

Arrange one rösti on each warmed plate, spread thickly with the dilled soured cream then top with slices of the seasoned salmon. Top each serving (if liked) with a teasp of caviar. Decorate with a sprig of dill and serve.

A Fantasy of Exotic Fruits with a Cassis and Fresh Ginger Dressing

S E R V E S   8

Serve at once

Select the fruits for their variety of colour, texture and flavour – you want to 'paint' a beautiful abstract picture on each plate: a slice each of a couple of the fruits, a handful of berries and grapes, a whole fig or physalis.

An assortment of fruits in season: physalis, mango, star fruit, fresh pineapple, sharon fruit, fresh figs, cherries, raspberries, seedless grapes

F O R   T H E   D R E S S I N G
1 tbsp finely grated lemon rind

1 tbsp each fresh orange and lemon juice

3 teasp Crème de Cassis or blackcurrant cordial

2 teasp raspberry or cider vinegar

5 tbsp sunflower oil

1 tbsp walnut oil

½ teasp salt

10 grinds black pepper

1 × 1 inch (2.5 cm) piece of fresh ginger, peeled and grated

F O R   T H E   G A R N I S H
8 tiny sprigs mint

seeds from 2 passion fruits

1 Put the dressing ingredients into a screw-top jar and shake until thickened, then refrigerate.

2 Half an hour before serving, prepare the fruit according to type.

T O   S E R V E

Arrange the fruit decoratively on fairly large plates and garnish with the mint and a scattering of passion fruit seeds. Spoon over the dressing, or pass it at the table for each guest to dress their own salad.

Indische Melone
(Melon in a Piquant Dressing)

SERVES 8

Prepared melon keeps 2 days, the dressing 2 weeks, under refrigeration

A Viennese speciality. Use melons of different colours for the most striking visual effect.

1 medium Ogen melon

1 Galia melon, firm but perfumed

1 Charentais melon (Cantaloupe)

FOR THE DRESSING
1 × 8 oz (225 g) jar redcurrant jelly, melted

5 fl oz (150 ml/⅔ cup) fresh orange juice (about 2 oranges)

2 fl oz (50 g/¼ cup) Kirsch or white rum

2 teasp Dijon mustard

2 level tbsp mango or peach chutney

10 grinds black pepper

FOR THE GARNISH
8 sprigs fresh mint or chervil

8 twists fresh lime

1 Early in the day (or the day before) scoop out the melons into balls, set in a sieve over a basin and leave to drip for 1 hour, then cover and chill. (This is essential to prevent juice leaching out of the melons, diluting the dressing.)

2 Whisk together all the ingredients for the dressing and refrigerate.

3 An hour before serving, add the melon balls to the dressing.

TO SERVE

Divide the melon and dressing between eight tall glasses and decorate with the herb sprigs and lime twists.

Salads

Orange, Watercress and Toasted Sunflower Seed Salad

Serves 6–8

Serve the day it is prepared

A light and refreshing starter to serve with a special bread such as olive, sun-dried tomato or nut.

2 bunches watercress, leaves only, or 12 oz (350 g) Belgian chicory (4–5 very small heads)

2 large or 4 medium thin-skinned oranges (seedless navels if possible)

FOR THE DRESSING
4 tbsp walnut oil

1 tbsp lemon juice

1 tbsp mint jelly, melted

½ teasp salt

8 grinds black pepper

FOR THE GARNISH
1 large chrysanthemum flower

2 tbsp toasted sunflower seeds

1 Wash and dry the watercress if necessary, or cut the ends off the chicory (if used) then separate the leaves.

2 Peel the oranges with a small serrated knife, removing the pith as well, and section them.

3 Add any free orange juice to the dressing ingredients and whisk well to form a slightly thickened emulsion.

4 Arrange the watercress or chicory and the orange sections in a bowl – a glass one for the prettiest effect.

TO SERVE

Just before serving, toss in the dressing and scatter with the chrysanthemum petals and the toasted sunflower seeds.

A Salad from San Francisco

S E R V E S   6 – 8

Dressing keeps 1 week. Dress salad just before serving

A stunning presentation, with both visual and taste appeal.

a nut of butter or margarine

2 teasp brown sugar

2 oz (50 g/½ cup) shelled pecans
(or walnuts)

2 × 7 oz (200 g) packs mixed
ready-prepared salad leaves

10 stalks fresh chives, each cut
into 3 inch (7.5 cm) lengths

8 oz (225 g) fresh raspberries or
strawberries, the latter quartered
if large

FOR THE DRESSING

2 tbsp walnut or hazelnut oil

4 tbsp sunflower oil

2 tbsp extra virgin olive oil

1 tbsp raspberry or red wine
vinegar

juice of ½ lemon (1½ tbsp)

1 teasp honey or soft brown sugar

1 teasp Moutarde de Meaux (or
English dried mustard powder)

1 pinch sea salt

10 grinds black pepper

1 Shake all the dressing ingredients together in a jar. Chill, preferably overnight.

2 In a small non-stick frying pan, melt the fat and sugar then add the pecans. Toss over moderate heat for 2–3 minutes until glazed then allow to cool.

3 Tear up the salad leaves and toss with enough dressing to coat. Arrange on individual plates with the chives, raspberries and pecans scattered decoratively on top.

T O   S E R V E

Serve chilled with pugliese bread or light rye bread.

A Spring Garland Salad with a Hazelnut Vinaigrette

SERVES 6–8

Use the salad the same day. Vinaigrette keeps 1 month under refrigeration

The 'garland' is composed of multi-coloured lettuces with tiny 'flowers' of yellow, red and orange scattered throughout. In the centre there may be a savoury tarte or crostini topped with Ginger-Spiked Chicken Liver Pâté (see page 14) or Bruschette hot from the oven (see page 21).

1 oak leaf lettuce and 1 × 7 oz (200 g) pack frisée (curly endive), or 2 × 7 oz (200 g) packs mixed greens (including oak leaf lettuce and frisée)

1 medium yellow pepper, seeded and cut in tiny dice

1–2 oz (25–50 g) sun-dried tomatoes, cut in tiny dice

8 physalis (Cape gooseberries), halved, paper coverings discarded

2 rounded tbsp honey-roasted cashews

FOR THE HAZELNUT VINAIGRETTE

4 tbsp white wine or cider vinegar

2 tbsp lemon juice

4 fl oz (125 ml) sunflower oil

3 tbsp hazelnut oil

1 fat clove garlic, crushed

2 level teasp caster sugar

1 teasp Dijon mustard

1 level teasp salt

1 Put all the vinaigrette ingredients into a large screw-top jar and shake together until thoroughly blended and thickened – about 1 minute. Leave at room temperature until required.

2 Finely tear the salad greens with the fingers. Put in a bowl with the pepper and tomato dice, and halved physalis, and toss with just enough dressing to coat the leaves lightly.

TO SERVE

Arrange in a 'garland' on each individual plate, scatter with the nuts and place the chosen 'starter' in the centre.

A Salad of Spring Leaves, Black Grapes and Toasted Seeds with a Creamy Blue Cheese Dressing

SERVES 6–8

Prepare and serve dressing and salad on the day

The sharp but creamily-textured dressing makes a pleasing contrast with the bland greens and the sweet grapes.

2 × 7 oz (200 g) packs crisp salad leaves

1 × 4½ oz (140 g) pack corn salad (lamb's lettuce)

4 oz (125 g) black seedless grapes

1 tbsp toasted sesame seeds, flaked hazelnuts or sunflower seeds

FOR THE DRESSING

4 fl oz (125 ml/½ cup) extra virgin olive oil

4 tbsp crème fraîche

1 tbsp lemon juice

1 oz (25 g/¼ cup) crumbled blue cheese (or more to taste)

¼ teasp sea salt

15 grinds black pepper

1 teasp caster sugar

1 Shake all the dressing ingredients together in a screw-top jar until emulsified. Leave for several hours.

2 Arrange the salad leaves and corn salad in a large bowl, stir in the grapes then chill.

TO SERVE

Toss the salad thoroughly with the dressing then arrange in a salad bowl or individual plates. Sprinkle with the toasted seeds or nuts.

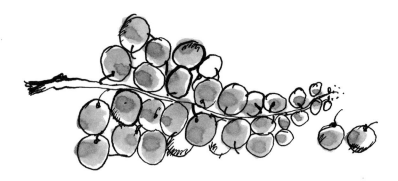

Chicory and Frisée Salad with Roquefort and Garlic Croûtons

SERVES 6–8

Prepare and serve dressing and salad on the day. Croûtons freeze 1 month

The accent is on 'crunch' in this richly flavoured salad dressed with garlic-scented croûtons.

2 × 7 oz (200 g) packs frisée (curly endive)

6 small heads Belgian chicory, cut lengthways into four

2 oz (50 g/½ cup) shelled pecans, lightly toasted or grilled

3 oz (75 g/¾ cup) crumbled Roquefort or other blue cheese, e.g. Lanarkshire Blue or mature Danish Blue

FOR THE CROÛTONS
4 fl oz (125 ml/½ cup) extra virgin olive oil

2 fat cloves garlic, finely sliced

4 thick slices white or brown bread, cut in ½ in (1.25 cm) cubes

salt

FOR THE DRESSING
2 tbsp fresh lemon juice

3 teasp white wine vinegar

garlic oil (see below)

½ teasp each of salt and caster sugar

10 grinds black pepper

1 Flavour the oil for the croûtons with the garlic by leaving them together for 2 hours then strain out the garlic, reserving the oil.
Preheat the oven to Gas 4 (350°F, 180°C).

2 Arrange the bread cubes in a shallow ovenproof tray, drizzle them with 2 tbsp of the garlic-flavoured oil and season with a little salt. Toss well to coat evenly then bake for 15 minutes until golden brown. Allow to cool.

3 To make the dressing, put the lemon juice and vinegar into a screw-top jar together with the remaining garlic oil, the salt, sugar and black pepper. Shake until slightly thickened.

4 An hour before serving, combine the frisée, chicory, pecans and cheese in a large bowl. Add the dressing and toss until all the ingredients are evenly coated.

TO SERVE
Turn into a wide salad bowl and scatter with the croûtons.

A Salad of Mixed Leaves, Physalis and Fresh Figs with a Zesty Ginger Vinaigrette

SERVES 6–8 AS A SIDE SALAD, 4 AS A STARTER

Serve the same day

An ideal plate-mate for the Bruschette (see page 21), or serve as a side salad with a main course.

1 × 7 oz (200 g) pack Continental-style salad leaves

2 Little Gem lettuces, cut in slim wedges

1 large ripe avocado, peeled, stoned and cut in crescents

1 × 3½ oz (100 g) pack physalis (Cape gooseberries), paper coverings discarded

4 fresh figs, cut in sixths

2 tbsp toasted pine kernels

FOR THE DRESSING

½ teasp grated lime rind

½ teasp grated orange rind

1 tbsp fresh lime juice

1½ tbsp orange juice

¼ teasp salt

8 grinds black pepper

1 scant teasp caster sugar

2 teasp grated fresh ginger

2 tbsp walnut oil

2½ tbsp extra virgin olive oil

1 Chill the salad greens and the wedges of Little Gem lettuce. Arrange the prepared fruit in a shallow dish.

2 In a screw-top jar, shake together all the dressing ingredients until thickened – 1 minute. Spoon over the fruit and leave to marinate for an hour.

TO SERVE

Arrange the salad greens on individual plates and spoon over the fruit and dressing. Scatter with the pine kernels. Serve with the Bruschette (see page 21) straight from the oven.

— Cook's Tip —
PHYSALIS BY ANY OTHER NAME

This small orange fruit – it's about the size of a large cherry – is also known as a Cape gooseberry or Chinese lantern. The flesh has a sharp, almost gooseberry flavour. You will sometimes see it in a smart restaurant coated with fondant amongst the petit four selection. It first rose to fame as a garnish during the era of nouvelle cuisine – now it's to be found on the shelves of most supermarkets.

A Tossed Green Salad with Marinated Kumquats in a Fruited Dressing

SERVES 6–8

Serve the same day

A light refreshing salad enlivened by the kumquats, whose natural acidity is softened by the gentle flavour of the nut oil. It makes an excellent starter or a mid-meal pause in the French manner.

6 oz (175 g) kumquats, quartered lengthways

1 lb (450 g) Belgian chicory

1 × 7 oz (200 g) pack frisée (curly endive)

2 oz (50 g/½ cup) pine kernels, toasted and lightly seasoned with fine sea salt

FOR THE DRESSING
3 fl oz (75 ml/⅓ cup) sunflower oil

1 fl oz (25 ml/2 tbsp) walnut or hazelnut oil

1 fl oz (25 ml/2 tbsp) raspberry vinegar

1 teasp fresh lemon juice

2 teasp sugar

1 teasp prepared wholegrain mustard

½ teasp salt

5 grinds black pepper

3 teasp chopped dill

1 Several hours in advance, make the dressing by shaking all the ingredients together in a screw-top jar until thickened. Pour into a container, add the quartered kumquats, cover and refrigerate.

2 Cut the stems from the chicory and discard any damaged outer leaves. Separate the leaves then arrange in a wide shallow salad bowl with the frisée. Cover and chill.

TO SERVE

Just before serving, shake the dressing again then pour on to the salad together with the kumquats and toss until the leaves are well coated and glistening. Sprinkle with the pine kernels.

Master Class Vinaigrette

The vinaigrette with onion and parsley keeps 3 days, without them 1 month

This is an excellent all-purpose dressing. There is a good oil/vinegar balance which is perfect for green salads but can always be sharpened if necessary with a little vinegar. We have found that a ratio of one part to three allows the olive oil content to flavour the dressing without overwhelming it, but you can alter the proportion or substitute a nut oil (walnut or hazelnut), or use only a flavourless oil such as sunflower or grapeseed instead.

9 fl oz (250 ml/1 cup + 2 tbsp) sunflower oil

3 fl oz (75 ml/⅓ cup) extra virgin olive oil

3 fl oz (75 ml/⅓ cup) wine vinegar

3 teasp lemon juice

3 teasp caster sugar or granular sweetener

1½ teasp sea salt

1½ teasp prepared wholegrain mustard

30 grinds black pepper

3 medium cloves garlic, halved (optional)

3 tbsp chopped parsley

1 small onion, finely chopped, or 3 oz/75 g spring onion bulbs or shallots, finely chopped

1 Put all the ingredients in a large screw-top jar or bowl and shake or whisk well until thickened.

2 Leave in the refrigerator to mature for several hours.

The Main Course

It makes good sense when time is limited to concentrate all the effort on an impressive main course.

Whether you choose fish, meat, poultry or vegetarian dishes from our repertoire, you'll find each one majors on the finest and freshest ingredients of the season, with flavour the main consideration. So, a fresh salmon strudel is teamed with basil, a Greek dish of lamb and caramelised shallots is spiced with cinnamon, roast duck is married with an apple and Drambuie sauce, a prime rib roast is given a coating of mixed peppercorns, and a juicy mixture of woodland mushrooms is combined with toasted pine kernels to make a luscious filling for a puff pastry slice.

FISH

Fillets of Salmon under a Crushed Pecan Crust

SERVES 6–8

At its best up to 1 hour after cooking, but will keep for 2 days under refrigeration

The delicate, slightly sweet flavour of the pecans marries to perfection with the salmon. The 'crust' it forms with the herbs and butter keeps the delicate flesh succulent and silky on the tongue.

1½–2 lb (675–900 g) salmon fillet, cut into 6–8 pieces

a little butter

salt and freshly ground white pepper

about 2–3 tbsp reduced-calorie mayonnaise

FOR THE CRUST
8 oz (225 g/2 cups) shelled pecans

4 tbsp very finely snipped fresh chives

1½ oz (40 g/3 tbsp) unsalted butter, melted

FOR THE GARNISH
segments of fresh lemon or lime

1 For the crust, grind the nuts until like coarse sand in the food processor, then mix with the chives and melted butter in a small bowl.

2 Lightly grease with butter a shallow tin wide enough to hold the pieces of salmon in one layer.

3 Arrange the salmon pieces in this dish and season lightly with salt and pepper. Spread the surface of each piece with a thin layer of mayonnaise and completely cover with the nut mixture, patting it firmly in place.

Preheat the oven to Gas 7 (425°F, 220°C).

4 Bake for 8–10 minutes, until the fish flakes easily with a fork and looks opaque.

TO SERVE
Serve straight from the oven or at room temperature.

SUGGESTED ACCOMPANIMENTS
When warm Creamed Potatoes in the Greek Style (see page 83) or baby new potatoes boiled then tossed in the same pan with a large nut of butter, heated until it turns a light golden brown, and a tbsp chopped parsley.

At room temperature Green salad and cucumber salad.

Grilled or Baked Fillets of Sea Bass or Salmon with a Citrus and Pistachio Sauce

SERVES 6

The fish is best eaten warm or at room temperature. Leftovers keep 2 days under refrigeration. Do not freeze. Sauce keeps 3 days under refrigeration.

The beautiful pale green sauce has a rich yet piquant flavour that blends well with the fish. (Don't be tempted to overcook the fish or it may become dry.)

6 × 4–5 oz (125–150 g) fillets of salmon, skinned

olive oil

salt and freshly ground black pepper

FOR THE SAUCE
1 × 3½ oz (100 g/scant 1 cup) natural shelled pistachios

2 tbsp lemon or lime juice

5 tbsp extra virgin olive oil

½ teasp salt

finely grated zest of 1 large orange

5 tbsp fresh orange juice (approx. 1 large orange)

FOR THE GARNISH
1 whole lemon, cut in 6 wedges

1 To start the sauce, using a food processor, process the pistachios until finely chopped.

2 Add all the remaining sauce ingredients and process until thickened but still with a little texture left. Pour into a jug. The sauce should be of a coating consistency – if too thick, thin with a little orange juice. Serve at room temperature.

The fish may be either grilled or baked.

3 To grill the fish, preheat the grill with the grill pan in place, lightly brushed with olive oil (about 3 minutes). Brush the fish with olive oil, sprinkle lightly with salt and pepper, then grill for 6 minutes until cooked to the centre.

4 To bake the fish, preheat the oven to Gas 8 (450°F, 230°C). Oil and season the fish as before, then bake for 8 minutes or until cooked through.

TO SERVE

Arrange the fish on individual plates, spoon over the sauce and serve garnished with the lemon wedges.

SUGGESTED ACCOMPANIMENT

Crusty country bread or ciabatta bread or rolls to mop up the wonderful sauce.

A Strudel of Fresh Salmon Perfumed with Basil and Served with Cacik

SERVES 8. MAKES 2 STRUDELS, EACH SERVING 4

The strudels are best served freshly baked. Leftovers keep 2 days under refrigeration

An unusual and utterly delectable way of serving salmon in pastry. Fillo pastry is sold ready-rolled so each strudel can be put together in minutes (see page 127 for notes on using filo pastry). The icy-cold, slightly tart sauce makes a refreshing contrast to the warm pastry and the mild flavour of the fish.

1½–1¾ lb (675–800 g) thick fillet of salmon on the skin

1 × 14 oz (140 g) (approx.) packet filo pastry (sheets measuring 18 × 12 inches/45 × 30 cm)

4½ oz (140 g/½ cup + 1 tbsp) unsalted butter, melted

3 fl oz (75 ml/⅓ cup) vermouth or dry sherry

1 oz (25 g/4 tbsp) fresh basil leaves

sea salt and freshly ground black pepper

FOR THE CACIK

1 large cucumber, thinly sliced

salt

10 fl oz (275 ml/1¼ cups) creamy fromage frais or Greek-style yoghurt

1 good pinch white pepper

1 clove garlic, crushed, or 1 teasp garlic purée

3 teasp white wine vinegar

1 good pinch sugar

1 tbsp finely snipped basil leaves

1 First make the cacik. Sprinkle the cucumber with salt and leave in a sieve for 30 minutes then rinse quickly and dab dry.

2 Stir together with all the other ingredients and chill for several hours.

3 Slice the salmon with a flexible knife on the diagonal, rather like smoked salmon – it should be ¼ inch (6 mm) thick.

Preheat the oven to Gas 6 (400°F, 200°C).

4 For each strudel you will need four sheets of filo pastry. (If the pastry is less than 18 inches/45 cm wide you will probably need to use 1½ sheets for each layer, overlapping them slightly so that the total width is approximately 18 inches/45 cm.) Use half the salmon, wine, basil and seasonings.

5 To make the first strudel, count out the four sheets and leave the remainder covered with a tea towel to prevent them drying out.

6 Brush each sheet in turn with an even layer of melted butter, laying them on top of each other to form a stack.

7 Leaving ½ inch (1.25 cm) at either side and 1 inch (2.5 cm) at the top edge clear, cover with the salmon slices. Season lightly with salt and a few grinds of black pepper. Sprinkle with the vermouth or sherry, then lay some shredded basil on top.

8 Turn in the ½ inch (1.25 cm) of clear pastry at either side then roll up into a strudel. Arrange on a well buttered baking sheet, join down.

9 Brush the strudel top with more of the melted butter. Make diagonal cuts through the top layer to indicate four portions.

I O Repeat with the further four sheets of pastry and the remaining ingredients to make the second strudel.

I I Bake the strudels for 15 minutes or until crisp and golden brown.

T O   S E R V E
Allow the strudels to cool for 10–15 minutes, then slice and serve with the cacik.

S U G G E S T E D   A C C O M P A N I M E N T S
A Stir-Fry of Baby Vegetables (see page 89) or A Salad of Spring Leaves with a Nut Oil and Balsamic Vinegar Dressing (see page 93).

A Whole Filleted Salmon Enclosing a Delicate Sole Mousse, Dilled Chantilly Mayonnaise

SERVES 6–8

Fish keeps 2 days under refrigeration. Freeze leftover fish 1 month. Sauce keeps 1 week under refrigeration. Do not freeze the sauce

This is a wonderfully pretty 'party piece', each pale pink slice of salmon revealing a centre of pale green mousse. The flavour is magnificent too! It can be served warm (15 minutes after cooking), but it slices to perfection only when allowed some time to set.

Note A 4½–5 lb (2–2.5 kg) fish will serve ten to twelve people, a 3½–4 lb (1.6–1.8 kg) fish will serve six to eight. The filling and the cooking time remain the same.

1 wild (or farmed) salmon, filleted and skinned

fine sea salt

8 fl oz (225 ml/1 cup), or 1 × 9 fl oz (250 ml) can dry white wine

FOR THE MOUSSE
8 oz (225 g) skinned and filleted lemon sole (or plaice if unavailable)

1 oz (25 g/⅓ cup) fresh dill

2 tbsp snipped fresh chives

2 tbsp chopped fresh parsley or chervil

1 teasp salt

1 good pinch white pepper

1 egg white

5 fl oz (150 ml/⅔ cup) chilled double or whipping cream

FOR THE DILLED CHANTILLY MAYONNAISE
4 fl oz (125 ml/½ cup) creamy (8% fat) fromage frais or crème fraîche

8 fl oz (225 ml/1 cup) mayonnaise

1 tbsp snipped dill

Preheat the oven to Gas 4 (350°F, 180°C).

1 For the mousee, cut the sole or plaice fillets into roughly 1 inch (2.5 cm) chunks, and put into the food processor. Snip the dill and the chives (most easily done with kitchen scissors). Put into the food processor along with the chopped parsley and seasonings, and process until puréed.

2 Add the egg white and cream and process only until creamily thickened – about 10 seconds.

3 Lightly oil a double thickness of foil large enough to parcel the salmon. Place in a large baking dish.

4 Place one salmon fillet on top of the foil, lightly salt then spread with an even layer of the mousse.

5 Lightly salt the second fillet and lay on top of the mousse, re-forming the fish.

6 Heat the wine until steaming (about 1 minute in the microwave), then pour over the fish and seal the foil into a loose parcel. (This allows the steam to circulate.)

7 Bake for 45 minutes then take out of the oven and leave for 15 minutes.

8 Carefully open the parcel and pour the fish juices into a container. Freeze for another use.

9 Re-seal the fish then leave until cool to the touch. Refrigerate until required, preferably overnight.

1 0 For the dilled chantilly mayonnaise, mix the ingredients gently but thoroughly together, then leave for 24 hours in the refrigerator.

T O   S E R V E
Unwrap the fish and cut it in slices. Serve with the chantilly mayonnaise.

S U G G E S T E D   A C C O M P A N I M E N T S
When warm   New potatoes and sugar snap peas.

At room temperature   A Salad of Artichoke Hearts with a Lemon and Tarragon Dressing (see page 92).

Délice of Salmon and Asparagus with a Delicate Tarragon and Lemon Sauce

S E R V E S 8

Serve the same day. Do not freeze

This elegant dish is especially easy to prepare in a domestic kitchen with the help of a microwave. Then, it is a very simple matter to get the degree of 'done-ness' just right. However it can also be steamed on top of the stove. The sweet/sour sauce is a good partner for any salmon dish – it's much lighter than mayonnaise or hollandaise. Blending the ingredients in the food processor before they are heated ensures the sauce thickens evenly without fear of curdling.

FOR THE DÉLICE
8 escalopes of salmon cut very thinly at an angle, like smoked salmon, each weighing 2½–3 oz (65–75 g) (a good 1½ lb/675 g fillet of fish before skinning)

32 spears fresh or frozen short spears of asparagus

salt and freshly ground white pepper

FOR THE SAUCE
15 fl oz (425 ml/2 cups) hot water with ¾ fish or vegetable stock cube

4 egg yolks

1 tbsp cornflour

3 tbsp fresh lemon juice

8 grinds black pepper

10 grinds sea salt

3 teasp caster sugar

1 tbsp chopped fresh tarragon

TO GARNISH
8 sprigs fresh tarragon

1 Under a piece of silicone paper, gently beat out each salmon escalope to a piece approximately 7 × 3 inches (17.5 × 7.5 cm). Some may need patching or trimming.

2 Blanch the asparagus only until 'al dente'. If pre-packed, for 1 minute less than packet directions.

3 Season the salmon and asparagus with salt and white pepper.

4 Take each escalope in turn, lay a spear of asparagus on the top and then roll up to cover most of the stem but leaving the tip showing. Do the same with 2 or 3 more spears, each turn of the salmon enclosing another spear, so that the délice has 3–4 spears according to size, rolled inside.

5 Repeat with the remaining escalopes and asparagus spears.

6 To cook in the microwave, lay four délices at a time in a microwave-safe dish, cover and cook for 2½ minutes in a 650 watt oven, 2 minutes in a 700 watt oven. Leave to stand for 3 minutes, then lift out carefully and drain on paper towels. Repeat with the remaining four délices.

7 To steam, arrange all the délices in a single layer in the upper section of the steamer, and steam for 4–5 minutes until opaque. Drain on paper towels.

8 When cool, cover and refrigerate.

9 To make the sauce, process all the ingredients in the food processor for 5 seconds until thoroughly mixed. Turn into a thick-based pan and stir over medium heat until the mixture comes to the boil, thickens and lightly coats the back of a wooden spoon. Stir in the tarragon. Chill.

T O   S E R V E

Arrange on individual plates and spoon over some of the sauce. Garnish with a sprig of tarragon.

S U G G E S T E D   A C C O M P A N I M E N T S

A French stick, crisped for 4 minutes in a moderate oven then cooled for 10 minutes before cutting in generous slices and buttering.

Sole Gratinée with a Curried Lemon Sauce

S E R V E S   6 – 8

Serve hot or cold. Keeps 2 days under refrigeration

This is one of those utterly simple dishes that can make your reputation as an innovative cook with a flair for unusual flavour combinations. Block fillets of sole are when the fish is cut into two fillets rather than four.

2 lb (900 g) block fillets of lemon sole or plaice, skinned then folded lengthways to make an even thickness

1 small bunch spring onion bulbs, or 2 large shallots, thinly sliced

1 fine lemon, thinly sliced

F O R   T H E   S A U C E
5 fl oz (150 ml/⅔ cup) soured cream

5 fl oz (150 ml/⅔ cup) mild mayonnaise

4 tbsp dry or medium dry sherry or vermouth

1 teasp mild curry paste

1½ tbsp lemon juice

F O R   T H E   G A R N I S H
6–8 sprigs fresh chervil

Preheat the oven to Gas 4 (350°F, 180°C).

1 For the sauce, stir together the soured cream, mayonnaise, sherry or vermouth, curry paste and lemon juice.

2 In a baking dish large enough to hold the fish in one layer, sprinkle the spring onion or shallots, then lay the fish on top.

3 Spoon the sauce evenly over the fish and arrange the halved slices of lemon decoratively on top.

4 Bake for 30-35 minutes or until the fish flakes.

T O   S E R V E
Serve from the baking dish, scattered with fresh chervil.

S U G G E S T E D   A C C O M P A N I M E N T S
When warm   Plain boiled potatoes with a scattering of parsley and coarse sea salt.

When cold   Warm sun-dried tomato bread.

Steaks of Tuna, Halibut or Sea Bass with a Provençale Sauce

SERVES 6

Serve hot off the grill. Leftovers keep 2 days under refrigeration

The hot sun of Provence and the perfumed carpet of wild herbs spread under the dusty olive trees that make walking such a delight, all seem to be captured in this fragrant but simple dish. A wonderful way to treat prime fish.

6 × 6 oz (175 g) steaks of fresh tuna, halibut or sea bass, each cut ¾ inch (2 cm) thick

1 medium onion, thinly sliced

2 bay leaves

6 tbsp extra virgin olive oil

½ teasp salt

15 grinds black pepper

½ oz (15 g) (1 handful) fresh marjoram, finely chopped

2 fat cloves garlic, crushed

a little olive oil for greasing

4 tbsp lemon juice

1 × 14 oz (400 g) can finely chopped tomatoes in concentrated tomato juice

1 teasp sugar

4 oz (125 g/1 cup) Provençale or Greek black olives, stoned, or 3 tbsp capers

FOR THE GARNISH
1 rounded tbsp chopped parsley

1 Lay the fish in one layer in a shallow dish.

2 In a small bowl, mix together the onion slices, bay leaves, olive oil, salt and pepper, marjoram and garlic, then spoon over the fish.

3 Marinate the fish steaks for at least 1 hour (longer will do no harm).

4 Remove the onion and bay leaves and discard.

5 Grease the grill pan with olive oil and put under a hot grill. After 2 minutes, arrange the fish steaks on top and brush well with the marinade.

6 Grill without turning for 8–10 minutes or until the fish flakes easily with a fork.

7 Meanwhile transfer the remaining marinade to a small pan and add the lemon juice, tomatoes, sugar and olives (or capers). Heat until bubbling and thick.

TO SERVE

Arrange the grilled fish on a warm platter or individual plates and spoon over the sauce. Sprinkle with the parsley and serve.

SUGGESTED ACCOMPANIMENT

A Salad of Sugar Snap Peas and Roasted Peppers with Cashews in a Basil Vinaigrette (see page 91).

Marinated Salmon Trout in a Muscat and Pine Kernel Sauce

SERVES 6–8

Serve at room temperature. Keeps 2 days under refrigeration

A first cousin once removed of the rather more plebeian Maqueraux au Vin Blanc, this is an elegant full-flavoured dish to serve for a summer luncheon or supper party. Muscat d'Alsace is a light dry white wine with a wonderfully grapey flavour which marries to perfection with the raisins. A white Sémillon could be substituted.

4 × 12 oz (350 g) salmon trout, filleted but skin left on and divided lengthways

salt

flour for coating

extra virgin olive oil

8 oz (225 g) shallots, finely chopped

1 fat clove garlic, finely chopped

1 tbsp chopped fresh tarragon, or 1 teasp freeze-dried

1 bay leaf

5 level tbsp muscatel raisins

4 tbsp pine kernels, lightly toasted

8 fl oz (225 ml/1 cup) Muscat d'Alsace wine

5 fl oz (150 ml/⅔ cup) white wine vinegar

10 fl oz (275 ml/1¼ cups) hot water with ⅔ fish stock cube

2 teasp sugar

1 teasp salt

15 grinds black pepper

1 Lightly season the fillets with salt and dust them with flour, patting off the excess.

2 Pour oil into a large frying pan to a depth of ¼ inch (6 mm). Heat the oil for 2–3 minutes or until you can feel steady heat on your hand held 2 inches (5 cm) above it. Sauté the fillets, skin side up first, for 2 minutes on each side, to seal the surface. As they are cooked, transfer them to a shallow glass baking dish, large enough to hold them in one layer. Pour off any remaining oil.

3 Wipe out the pan then heat 2½ tbsp oil as before and in it cook the shallots and garlic, stirring until the shallots are softened.

4 Add all the remaining ingredients, bring to the boil and simmer uncovered for 10 minutes.

5 Discard the bay leaf and pour the mixture over the fish.

6 Let the fish marinate, covered and chilled, for 24–36 hours.

TO SERVE

Leave the fish at room temperature for 1 hour, then serve with some of the marinade spooned around it.

SUGGESTED ACCOMPANIMENT

Slices of buttered mixed grain bread to mop up the wonderful juices.

Rainbow Trout with Clementines, Dill and Fresh Strawberries

SERVES 6–8

Leftovers keep 2 days under refrigeration

This is an especially pretty presentation, with a mouth-watering combination of fish, fruit and delicate herb.

6–8 split fillets cut from 3–4 × 12–14 oz (350–400 g) whole rainbow trout

salt

FOR THE TOPPING
2 tbsp light soy sauce

2 tbsp fresh orange juice

1 tbsp extra virgin olive oil

1 tbsp sun-dried tomato paste (crema di pomodoro)

1 tbsp finely chopped parsley

1 clove garlic, finely chopped

2 teasp Worcestershire sauce

2 teasp lemon juice

15 grinds black pepper

FOR THE CLEMENTINE AND STRAWBERRY SALAD
1 tbsp caster sugar

1 tbsp boiling water

2 tbsp raspberry vinegar

10 grinds black pepper

1 tbsp chopped dill

6–8 clementines, peeled and sectioned

1 small punnet (8 oz/225 g) strawberries, sliced

1 hearted lettuce (Little Gem or iceberg), cut in slim sections

1 Wash and lightly salt the trout fillets then lay side by side in a heatproof dish suitable for grilling.

2 Mix together all the topping ingredients then spoon over the fish in an even layer. Allow to marinate at room temperature for 1 hour.

3 To start the salad, put the sugar in a small bowl, add the boiling water and stir until dissolved then stir in the vinegar, black pepper and dill.

4 Pour over the clementine sections in a shallow dish and leave for an hour at least, but overnight will do no harm.

5 Grill the fish 4 inches (10 cm) from a hot grill for 6–8 minutes or until the fish flakes easily and is firm to the touch. Serve hot off the grill or at room temperature.

6 Shortly before serving, slice the strawberries into a bowl, add the drained clementines and enough dressing to moisten both fruits, and mix gently together.

TO SERVE
Arrange a grilled fillet on each plate with some of the fruit, on a bed of lettuce.

SUGGESTED ACCOMPANIMENTS
Creamy mashed potatoes or Cyprus (small baking) potatoes baked to crunchiness in a regular oven or combination microwave.

Smoked Salmon Tart

SERVES 6

Serve the same day. Leftovers keep 2 days under refrigeration

This is more like a savoury cheesecake than the typical custard quiche. The combination of the slightly textured pastry, smooth filling and oaky smoked salmon is irresistible! If you don't want to make your own pastry, use 8 oz (225 g) bought shortcrust pastry with ½ teasp strong curry powder rolled into the top surface.

8 oz (225 g) Brown Herb Pastry (see page 126), substituting ½ teasp strong curry powder for the herbs and other flavourings

FOR THE FILLING
8 oz (225 g) frozen leaf spinach, defrosted and coarsely chopped (optional)

1 nut butter

1 pinch grated nutmeg

1 pinch salt

8 oz (225 g/1 cup) curd or ricotta cheese

2 teasp cornflour

3 egg yolks

1 whole egg

5 fl oz (150 ml/⅔ cup) whipping cream

1 teasp lemon rind

15 grinds black pepper

FOR THE GARNISH
8 oz (225 g) sliced smoked salmon (at room temperature), cut in neat pieces

1 × 9 oz (250 g/1 cup + 2 tbsp) carton Greek yoghurt or soured cream

2 tbsp snipped dill

Preheat the oven to Gas 6 (400°F, 200°C).

1 Roll the chilled dough into a circle 11–12 inches (35–40 cm) in diameter then ease into a loose-bottomed quiche tin 9–10 inches (25–30 cm) in diameter. Press it well into the sides, and trim off any excess. Prick the case all over with a fork, then line with a piece of foil pressed into its shape.

2 Bake the case for 10 minutes or until the pastry feels dry to the touch then remove the foil and bake for a further 5 minutes until lightly brown.

Reduce the oven temperature to Gas 5 (375°F, 190°C).

3 Meanwhile, put the spinach (if used) into a small frying pan and heat gently until all the free liquid has evaporated. Stir in the butter, nutmeg, and a pinch of salt.

4 Put the cheese into a bowl and add the remaining ingredients in the order given, using a balloon whisk to ensure it is smooth.

5 When ready to bake, lay the spinach on the base of the cooked case then pour on the cheese filling. Bake for 30 minutes or until puffed and golden, then remove.

6 Lay the salmon pieces on top, then drizzle with 2 rounded tbsp of the Greek yoghurt, and sprinkle with the dill.

Serve 5 minutes after baking, or later the same day, cut in wedges. Pass round the remaining yoghurt or soured cream.

S U G G E S T E D   A C C O M P A N I M E N T S
Asparagus Salad in the Italian Style (see page 94), accompanied by slices of buttered ficelle – the ultra-slim French bread that's almost all crust. For the ultimate in crunch, reheat the bread 3–4 minutes in the oven with the tart.

Fish in Tahina Sauce

S E R V E S   8

Keeps 2 days under refrigeration

This is our version of the classic Middle Eastern dish, *Samak B'Tarator*. The unusual sauce transforms baked fish into something rich and rare.

2 lb (900 g) sea bream fillets (or thick lemon sole or haddock), cut in 3½ oz (100 g) serving portions

salt and freshly ground black pepper

sunflower oil

4 oz (125 g) shallots, finely chopped

2 cloves garlic, finely chopped

F O R   T H E   T A H I N A   S A U C E
8 fl oz (225 ml/1 cup) bottled or canned light coloured tahina (sesame seed paste)

4 fl oz (125 ml/½ cup) lemon juice

4 fl oz (125 ml/½ cup) water

½ teasp salt

2 cloves garlic, crushed

1 large handful parsley (about ½ oz/15 g) coarsely chopped

Preheat the oven to Gas 6 (400°F, 200°C).

1 Arrange the fish in an ovenproof dish large enough to hold it in one layer.

2 Sprinkle the fish with salt and pepper then brush all over with oil. Cover loosely with silicone or greaseproof paper, and bake for 15–20 minutes or until it flakes easily with a fork.

3 Meanwhile sauté the shallots and garlic in 1½ tbsp oil until golden.

4 The sauce can be made earlier in the day. Slowly whisk the tahina, lemon juice, water, salt and garlic together until smooth – it should be of coating consistency. If too thick add a little water; if too thin, a little more tahina. Stir in half the parsley.

T O   S E R V E
As soon as the fish comes out of the oven, strew it with the shallots and garlic mixture then pour over the sauce, scatter with the remaining parsley and serve.

S U G G E S T E D   A C C O M P A N I M E N T
A good ready-to-serve tabbouleh (available at deli counters) and warm pitta bread.

MEAT

Master Class Moussaka

SERVES 8–10

Keeps 2 days under refrigeration. Freeze 1 month

It may not be traditional to use coconut milk instead of regular milk, or to grill the aubergines instead of frying them, for this great Greek classic, but it does produce a wonderfully light and digestible dish that's ideal for an informal lunch or supper (you can't taste the coconut). The moussaka reheats well.

2½ lb (1.1 kg) aubergines

olive oil

FOR THE MEAT MIXTURE
1 large onion, finely chopped

1 tbsp extra virgin olive oil

1 lb (450 g) lean lamb, finely minced

8 fl oz (225 ml/1 cup) red wine

1 × 14 oz (140 g) can finely chopped tomatoes in concentrated tomato juice

1 teasp honey

1 bunch fresh parsley, finely chopped (reserve 1 tbsp for garnish)

8 fl oz (225 ml/1 cup) hot water with ½ chicken or vegetable stock cube

2 teasp dried oregano

2 teasp ground cinnamon

½ teasp salt

15 grinds black pepper

FOR THE SAUCE
4 oz (125 g/½ cup) butter or margarine

3 oz (75 g/¾ cup) plain flour

1 × 14 fl oz (400 ml) can coconut milk

2 fl oz (50 ml/¼ cup) water

1 teasp grated nutmeg

5 large eggs

salt and freshly ground black pepper

FOR THE TOPPING
6 rounded tbsp fresh breadcrumbs

2 tbsp extra virgin olive oil

1 Trim off the ends of the aubergines and cut in ¼ inch (6 mm) thick slices. Brush lightly on both sides with olive oil and grill until golden brown.

2 For the meat mixture, sauté the onion gently in the olive oil in a heavy frying pan until soft and golden. Add the meat and cook more briskly until brown, using a large fork to break up any lumps.

3 Add the wine and bubble until reduced by half. Add the tomatoes and honey, then simmer uncovered for 10 minutes. Leaving 1 tbsp of parsley for garnish, stir in the rest together with the stock, oregano, cinnamon and salt and pepper.

4 Simmer uncovered for 30 minutes until almost no liquid remains. Taste and re-season if necessary.

5 To make the sauce, melt the fat, add the flour and cook, stirring, until the roux turns a pale fawn colour. Whisk in the coconut milk plus water and nutmeg. Bubble for 2 minutes, then take off the heat.

6 Whisk the eggs to blend well then gradually whisk into the sauce. Season to taste with salt and pepper.

Preheat the oven to Gas 4 (350°F, 180°C).

7 Arrange a quarter of the aubergine slices in the bottom of an oval or rectangular gratin dish, about 2½–3 inches (6.25–7.5 cm) deep and 11 inches (27.5 cm) long. Smooth a third of the meat mixture on top, and spread 4 tbsp of the sauce on top of the meat. Cover with two more layers of aubergine, meat and sauce, then cover with the remaining aubergine. Scatter evenly with the fresh breadcrumbs moistened with the oil and bake, uncovered, for 1 hour.

TO SERVE
Sprinkle with the reserved parsley, leave to 'set' for 10 minutes then cut in squares.

Patsas of Lamb with Caramelised Shallots and Muscatel Raisins, Jasmine Rice

SERVES 6

Keeps 3 days under refrigeration. Freeze 1 month (but spices may fade)

So good to come home to – a simple but subtly spiced casserole, the meat meltingly tender.

6–8 lamb neck steaks, approx.
6 oz (175 g) each

1½ tbsp extra virgin olive oil

1 teasp ground cinnamon

1 teasp ground ginger or 1 teasp ginger purée

1 tbsp light Muscovado (brown) sugar

hot chicken or vegetable stock to cover the meat (about
15 fl oz/425 ml/2 cups hot water with 1 stock cube)

1 teasp salt

20 grinds black pepper

1 tbsp chopped fresh or frozen parsley

1 tbsp chopped fresh coriander or 1 teasp freeze-dried

1 pinch saffron powder

1 clove garlic, finely chopped, or 1 teasp garlic purée

2 teasp tomato purée

2 teasp cornflour mixed with 2 tbsp cold water (if necessary)

3 oz (75 g/½ cup + 1 tbsp) Muscatel raisins

FOR THE CARAMELISED SHALLOTS
1½ tbsp extra virgin olive oil

12 oz (350 g) shallots (or pickling onions)

1 tbsp light Muscovado (brown) sugar

3 teasp ground cinnamon

2 teasp ground cumin

FOR THE GARNISH
12 oz (350 g/2 cups) Thai jasmine rice or Basmati rice

1 In a flameproof sauté pan or casserole, heat the first 1½ tablespoons of oil, then add the meat. Sprinkle with the cinnamon, ginger and sugar, and cook briskly until a rich brown.

2 Lower the heat and barely cover with the hot stock, then stir in the salt, pepper, parsley, coriander, saffron, garlic and tomato purée.

3 Cover and simmer very gently for 1 hour on top of the stove or for 1½ hours in the oven preheated to Gas 2 (300°F, 150°C). Stir occasionally.

4 Meanwhile, for the shallots put the oil in an 8 inch (20 cm) sauté pan. Add the shallots, sprinkle with the sugar, and cook, covered, until they have softened and are beginning to colour, then add the spices. Uncover and continue to cook until a rich golden brown.

[*continues*]

5 When the meat is tender, thicken the sauce if necessary by stirring in the cornflour mixture. Spoon the shallots on top and cook, covered, for a further 20 minutes. Stir in the raisins.

6 Cook the rice according to packet directions.

T O   S E R V E
Either serve from the casserole with rice on the side, or arrange a bed of the rice on a heated platter and spoon the meat and shallots on top.

S U G G E S T E D   A C C O M P A N I M E N T
To contrast with the richness of the casserole, serve a Salad of Spring Leaves with a Nut Oil and Balsamic Vinegar Dressing (see page 93) or Spiced Kumquats (see page 96).

F A C I N G   P A G E   5 0 ,   T O P   T O   B O T T O M
A Strudel of Fresh Salmon Perfumed with Basil, served with a bowl of Cacik (page 36), *Delice of Salmon and Asparagus with a Delicate Tarragon and Lemon Sauce* (page 40)

O P P O S I T E
Patsas of Lamb with Caramelised Shallots and Muscatel Raisins served with Jasmine Rice (page 50) *and Spiced Kumquats* (page 96)

Roast Lamb Perfumed with Rosemary and Garlic, on a Bed of Braised Shallots and Potatoes

SERVES 6–8

Leftovers keep 3 days under refrigeration. Freeze 3 months

Shoulder of lamb is considered by connoisseurs to be the sweetest lamb joint of all. Here the rather neutral flavour of the meat is enhanced by spiking it with rosemary and garlic in the Provençale way. As the lamb cooks, the juices ooze out from these spike holes, giving a wonderful flavour to the vegetables cooking below. A leg of lamb can be treated in the same way.

3½ lb (1.6 kg) boned and rolled shoulder of lamb

2 large sprigs rosemary

2 large cloves garlic, slivered

TO COAT THE LAMB
20 grinds black pepper

extra virgin olive oil

1 teasp dry mustard

1 tbsp flour

2 tbsp demerara sugar

TO COOK BENEATH THE LAMB
2½ lb (1.1 kg) small new potatoes, scrubbed

1 teasp salt

1 lb (450 g) shallots

1 pint (575 ml/2½ cups) hot water with 1½ meat stock cubes

FOR THE SAUCE
juices from the roasting tin made up to 10 fl oz (275 ml/1¼ cups) with hot water

3 teasp cornflour

3½ fl oz (100 ml) red wine

Preheat the oven to Gas 4 (350°F, 180°C).

1 Several hours in advance or even the night before, use a small pointed knife to pierce the lamb at 2 inch (5 cm) intervals. Into each incision push a tiny sprig of rosemary and a sliver of garlic.

2 When ready to cook, grind black pepper over the lamb, brush with a thin layer of olive oil, and sprinkle with the mixed mustard and flour. Arrange on a rack that will fit 2 inches (5 cm) above a roasting tin.

3 Put the new potatoes into a pan of cold water, add the salt and bring slowly to the boil. Lift out with a slotted spoon, pat dry and arrange in the roasting tin.

4 In the same water, bring the shallots to the boil, then turn into a sieve and drench with cold water. The skins can now be easily removed. Arrange with the potatoes in the roasting tin.

5 Pour the stock over and around the potatoes and shallots.

6 Lay the meat on its rack on top of the vegetables, put in the oven and cook for 2¼ hours.

7 After 1 hour, take out the roasting tin and lift off the meat on its rack so that you can stir the vegetables. Replace the meat, sprinkle with the brown sugar, and return to the oven. Check after half an hour and if the stock seems to be drying up, add a little hot water.

8 Lift the meat out on to a dish and leave to stand, loosely covered with foil, or leave in the oven turned to its lowest setting. Lift the vegetables out with a slotted spoon and put into a dish. Cover and keep warm.

9 To make the sauce, put the roasting tin on the stove, add the boiling water then stir well to release all the delicious sediment. Mix the cornflour to a smooth cream with the wine and add to the pan. Bubble for 3 minutes, stirring well, and taste and re-season if necessary. (At this stage you may wish to transfer the sauce to a small pan to keep it hot.)

To serve
Allow the meat to stand for 20 minutes before slicing and serving, with the potatoes and shallots and the sauce offered separately.

Suggested Accompaniment
Minted peas or sautéed courgettes.

A Ragoût of Lamb with an Orange Liqueur Sauce

SERVES 6

Keeps 2 days under refrigeration. Freeze 3 months

The oranges add a refreshing touch to this light yet satisfying casserole.

2½ lb (1.1 kg) boneless lamb (leg or shoulder), cut in 2 × 1 inch (5 × 2.5 cm) chunks

2 tbsp flour seasoned with 1 teasp salt and 15 grinds black pepper

2 tbsp extra virgin olive oil

1 medium onion (5 oz/150 g), finely chopped

12 oz (350 g) shallots

2 teasp medium brown sugar

8 oz (225 ml/1 cup) dry white wine

10 fl oz (275 ml/1¼ cups) hot water with ¾ chicken stock cube

1 teasp salt

10 grinds black pepper

3 large navel oranges

2 teasp cornflour mixed with 2 tbsp cold water

4 tbsp orange-flavoured liqueur (Cointreau, Grand Marnier or Curaçao)

FOR THE GARNISH
1 tbsp chopped coriander (or parsley)

reserved orange sections

2 oz (50 g/½ cup) toasted broken cashews

Preheat the oven to Gas 2 (300°F, 150°C). The meat can be cooked completely in an oven-to-table casserole, or sautéed in a pan first.

I Shake the meat with the seasoned flour in a large plastic bag, pat off any excess, then lightly sauté in the oil in two batches. When the meat is a rich brown, lift out on to a plate using a slotted spoon.

2 Add the onion to the pan together with the shallots, sprinkle with the brown sugar and continue to cook over medium heat until the onion is golden brown.

3 Add the wine to the pan, stir well to incorporate any flavoursome bits on the bottom, then bubble for 3 minutes to concentrate the flavour.

4 Add the meat, the hot stock and seasoning, and bring slowly to the boil.

5 Meanwhile with a zester or grater remove shreds of peel from one orange, and reserve. Peel all the oranges, removing all the pith. Cut between the sections to release the fruit then reserve twelve sections for garnish. Add the remaining sections to the meat together with any juice that can be squeezed out of the orange 'skeletons' plus the orange peel shreds.

6 When the casserole is bubbling, cover it and transfer to the oven, then cook until the meat is very tender – about 1½ hours.

7 Stir in the dissolved cornflour and the liqueur, stir well, then simmer in the oven, covered, for a further 20 minutes.

TO SERVE
Either transfer to a platter or serve straight from the casserole, sprinkled with the herb and garnished with the orange sections and nuts.

SUGGESTED ACCOMPANIMENTS
Noodles and Parsnip and Orange Purée (see page 90).

Lamb Izmir

SERVES 6–8

Keeps 2 days under refrigeration. Freeze 3 months

A gently spiced casserole in the Turkish style with the aubergines giving it a distinctive flavour.

1½ lb (675 g) aubergines, cut in ¾ inch (2 cm) slices

sunflower oil for brushing

2½ lb (1.1 kg) boned-out lamb, cut in 2 inch (5 cm) chunks

2 tbsp extra virgin olive oil

1 large (8 oz/225 g) onion, finely chopped

1 fat clove garlic, chopped, or 1 teasp garlic purée

18 fl oz (525 ml/2¼ cups) hot water with 1 vegetable stock cube

2 level tbsp tomato purée

2 teasp brown sugar

½ teasp salt

10 grinds black pepper

1 teasp ground cumin

1½ teasp ground cinnamon

Preheat the oven to Gas 2 (300°F, 150°C).

1 Brush the aubergines with sunflower oil on both sides then grill until golden brown and tender when pierced with a pointed knife.

2 In a large frying or sauté pan brown the lamb quickly on both sides in the extra virgin olive oil. Lift out with a slotted spoon and drain on kitchen towels.

3 In the same oil, cook the onion over moderate heat until a rich golden brown, then add all the remaining ingredients (except the aubergines). Stir well and bring to the boil. Simmer uncovered for 5 minutes.

4 Put the meat in an oven-to-table casserole, pour over the bubbling sauce and cook in the slow oven for 1½ hours.

5 Add the aubergine slices to the casserole, cover and cook for 30 minutes.

TO SERVE
Bring the casserole to the table and serve straight on to the hot plates.

SUGGESTED ACCOMPANIMENT
Bulgur and Pine Kernel Pilaff (see page 81) and Spiced Kumquats (see page 96).

Daube of Beef with Hazelnut Dumplings

SERVES 6

Keeps 3 days under refrigeration. Freeze 3 months

A wonderful example of 'Cuisine Grandmère' – a simple, satisfying dish that depends on depth of flavour rather than elegant presentation for its appeal.

2 tbsp extra virgin olive oil

2½ lb (1.1 kg) braising steak, cut into 2 inch (5 cm) chunks

2 large onions sliced

2 level teasp brown sugar

the white part of a fat leek, diced

1 large carrot, diced

2 level teasp salt

10 grinds black pepper

1 teasp ground ginger

2 teasp each of dry mustard and flour

8 fl oz (225 ml/1 cup) red wine

hot meat stock (about 15 fl oz/425 ml/2 cups hot water with 1 stock cube)

FOR THE DUMPLINGS

1½ oz (40 g/3 tbsp) margarine

4 oz (125 g/1 cup) self-raising flour

1 oz (25 g/¼ cup) ground hazelnuts

2 teasp chopped parsley

½ teasp salt

10 grinds black pepper

1 egg

2 tbsp water

1 Heat the oil in a heavy sauté or frying pan, put in the meat (in two or three batches), and cook over high heat until a rich brown. Remove to a plate.

2 Add to the pan the sliced onions and brown sugar, the diced leek and carrot, and cook until a rich brown juice flows from the mixture – about 5 minutes.

3 Sprinkle in the salt, pepper, ginger, flour and mustard, stir well, then add the wine. Bubble for 3 minutes to concentrate the flavour. Return the meat to the pan then add just enough hot stock to barely cover the mixture. Stir well.

4 Cover and simmer on top of the stove or in the oven preheated to Gas 2 (300°F, 150°C) for 2½ hours (making sure that the liquid only shivers rather than bubbles), or until the meat is bite tender.

5 Meanwhile, make the dumplings by rubbing the fat into the flour until no piece larger than a small pea comes to the surface when the bowl is shaken. Add the ground hazelnuts, parsley and seasonings and mix thoroughly. Mix to a sticky dough with the egg and water.

6 After the meat has been cooking for 2 hours, uncover and, using a wet spoon, drop tablespoons of the mixture on to the simmering stew. Cover and continue to cook for the remaining 30 minutes.

Serve straight from the casserole.

S U G G E S T E D   A C C O M P A N I M E N T
Regular mashed potatoes or Creamed Potatoes in the Greek Style (the cheese can be omitted) (see page 83).

Keftethes with Aubergine

S E R V E S   6 – 8

Keeps 3 days under refrigeration. Freeze raw or cooked 3 months

The grilled aubergines give the meatballs a sweet and smoky flavour and make their texture light yet juicy.

1½ lb (675 g) aubergines, peeled and sliced ⅜ inch (1 cm) thick	1 medium onion, grated
sunflower oil	1 egg, beaten
1 lb (450 g) lean raw minced beef	2 heaped tbsp (approx.) porridge oats or ground rice
1½ teasp salt	flour for coating
20 grinds black pepper	

1 Brush each aubergine slice with some sunflower oil on both sides then arrange in a grill pan. Grill until golden on both sides. Chop to a rough purée.

2 Put the meat in a large bowl then add the salt and pepper, the aubergine purée, the onion, egg and the oats or ground rice. At this stage leave it for 30 minutes (or up to 2 hours) to firm up.

3 Thickly coat a plate with flour then with wetted hands take some of the meat mixture and form into 'golf balls' between the palms of the hands. Drop into the flour and coat lightly.

4 Fry the meatballs very gently in shallow sunflower oil until crisp on the outside and cooked right through – about 10 minutes. (They may be reheated in the microwave or by tossing in the pan.)

T O   S E R V E

Hot Arrange on a bed of mashed potatoes, rice or bulgur.

Cold Make smaller balls to spear with a cocktail stick and serve with drinks.

S U G G E S T E D   A C C O M P A N I M E N T

Bulgur and Vermicelli Pilav (see page 80).

Tournedos of Beef in Filo Pastry with a Rich Wine Sauce

SERVES 6–8

Serve freshly cooked

This is our simplified version of the dish served to a conference of G7 ministers and passed on to us by a friend with access to the corridors of European power! Entrecôte (eye-of-the-rib) steak can be used instead of fillet steak, if preferred.

6–8 × 4–6 oz (125–175 g) fillet steaks, well trimmed

15 grinds black pepper

2 tbsp extra virgin olive oil

salt

5 oz (150 g) shallots or 1 medium onion, finely chopped

2 teasp freeze-dried fines herbes

2 oz (50 g/½ cup) black olives (weight when stoned), chopped, or 8 oz (225 g/2½ cups) mushrooms, finely chopped

4 oz (125 g) any smooth liver pâté or liver sausage

1 × 14 oz (400 g) pack filo pastry

4 oz (125 g/½ cup) butter or margarine, melted

6–8 × 3 inch (7.5 cm) circles cut from 6–8 slices white or brown bread

1 tbsp each of poppy seeds and sesame seeds

FOR THE WINE SAUCE
15 fl oz (425 ml/2 cups) hot water with 1¼ beef stock cubes

1 carrot, chopped

½ onion, chopped

1 fat stick celery, chopped

10 fl oz (275 ml/1¼ cups), or 1 × 9 fl oz (250 ml) can fruity red wine

1 large sprig parsley

1 small bay leaf

1 teasp each tomato purée and brown sugar

2 teasp cornflour

The sauce can be made one or two days in advance, as follows.

1 Put all the ingredients except the cornflour into a pan, bring to the boil, partially cover and simmer for 30 minutes to concentrate the flavour.

2 Lift out the bay leaf and sprig of parsley, then purée the liquid and vegetables in a blender or food processor. (It may be frozen or refrigerated at this point.)

3 Put the cornflour into a bowl and mix to a cream with 2 tbsp water. Add to the sauce, bring to the boil and simmer for 3 minutes until smooth and glossy.

The sauce can now be reheated when required.

The steaks can be prepared earlier in the day but should be served almost straight from the oven.

4 Dry the steaks thoroughly and sprinkle both sides with some of the black pepper.

5 Heat a tbsp of the oil in a sauté pan, add the steaks and fry over moderate heat until brown on all sides. Remove from the pan, season lightly with salt and allow to cool.

6 Heat the remaining oil, add the shallot or onion (and mushrooms if used) and cook gently until softened. Add the dried herbs. Allow to cool slightly before mixing in the chopped olives (if used) and the pâté. Taste and add salt (if needed) and the remaining pepper.

7 Cut the filo into 18 to 24 × 10–11 inch (25–27.5 cm) squares. For each serving, stack three squares on top of each other, brushing each square in turn with melted fat. Divide the pâté mixture between each steak, spreading it evenly. Lay a circle of bread in the centre of each stack of pastry, lay a prepared steak on top, then gather the pastry into a purse, twisting it to close. Brush each purse with fat and sprinkle with the mixed seeds.

Preheat the oven to Gas 6 (400°F, 200°C).

8 Arrange the purses well apart on a lightly greased baking sheet and bake for 15 minutes until a rich golden brown.

TO SERVE
Serve with the sauce.

SUGGESTED ACCOMPANIMENTS
Parsnip and Orange Purée (see page 90) or Lemon Bulgur Timbales (see page 78).

— *Cook's Tip* —
BROWNING MEAT
Meat can be browned to perfection in a pan that's only been lightly brushed with oil, providing you wait until it has loosened itself before attempting to turn it. Brush the empty sauté pan with olive oil (which promotes better browning than vegetable oils) then put over moderate heat until you can feel the warmth on your palm held 2 inches (5 cm) above it. Cook the meat briskly on the first side – but only when you can lift it without sticking will it be brown enough to turn and cook the second side. This method is equally successful with meat balls.

Prime Ribs of Beef with a Crushed Three-Pepper Coating

S E R V E S   8 – 1 0

Leftovers keep 3 days under refrigeration. Freeze 3 months

The rib of beef nearest to the sirloin is perhaps the juiciest cut of all. This method of cooking produces a dark brown crusty outside, whilst the beef remains pink and juicy inside. Make sure that the joint has been hung for at least 10 days. It should also have its bones chined so that the joint will stand evenly in the roasting tin.

1 × 3 rib first cut joint of beef (also known as 'wing rib')

2 teasp black peppercorns

2 teasp green peppercorns

2 teasp Sichuan peppercorns

2 small sprigs fresh thyme (leaves stripped from stalks)

½ teasp sea salt

2 tbsp (approx.) extra virgin olive oil

8 oz (225 g) shallots or small onions

FOR THE SAUCE

5 fl oz (150 ml/⅔ cup) dry red wine, e.g. Burgundy or Côtes du Rhône

15 fl oz (425 ml/2 cups) good beef stock

2 teasp Dijon mustard and 2 teasp cornflour mixed with 2 tbsp cold water

salt and freshly ground black pepper

Leave the meat at room temperature for 1 hour. Preheat the oven to its highest temperature.

1 In a mortar (or strong small bowl) crush the three types of peppercorns, the thyme and the sea salt with the pestle or the end of a rolling pin.

2 Brush the meat lightly with the olive oil, then rub with the pepper mixture.

3 Place in the very hot oven for 30 minutes, then turn the temperature down to moderate, Gas 4 (350°F, 180°C) and continue to cook for a further 1½ hours (149°F/65°C on a meat thermometer). Baste the meat at half-hour intervals.

4 About 20 minutes before the meat is cooked, add the shallots to the roasting tin, turning them so they are coated with the juices.

5 Lift the cooked meat on to a carving dish, cover lightly with foil and leave in a warm place (either a warming oven or the back of the stove) for 20–30 minutes before carving. Remove the shallots with a slotted spoon and keep hot.

6 To make the sauce, skim as much fat as possible from the surface of the roasting tin. Place the tin over moderate heat, pour in the wine, then stir well with a wooden spoon to deglaze the pan. When all the delicious caramelised and crusty bits have been stirred into the wine, bubble for 2 minutes then turn into a small saucepan. Add the meat stock and simmer for 5 minutes, then stir in the mustard and cornflour liquid. Bubble for 30 seconds until thickened and glossy. Season to taste with salt and pepper.

TO SERVE
Carve fairly thickly, and serve with the shallots. Pass the sauce separately.

SUGGESTED ACCOMPANIMENT
Parsnip and Walnut Purée (see page 90) and roast potatoes.

Albondigas

SERVES 6 GENEROUSLY

Cooked meatballs keep 4 days under refrigeration. Freeze 3 months

Originally Spanish in origin, this version has a decidedly Mexican accent which transforms common or garden meatballs into a party dish.

FOR THE MEATBALLS

1½ lb (675 g) lean minced beef

2 oz (50 g/6 tbsp) raisins

1 medium onion

3 large 1 inch/2.5 cm thick slices brown or white bread

2 eggs

1 teasp salt

10 grinds black pepper

2 teasp chopped fresh coriander or parsley

FOR THE SAUCE

1 large (8–9 oz/225–250 g) onion, finely chopped

2 tbsp olive oil

1 large red pepper, seeded and cut in ½ inch (1.25 cm) squares

1 fat clove garlic, chopped, or 1 teasp garlic purée

4 tbsp Amontillado (medium dry) sherry

1 × 5 oz (150 g) can tomato purée

8 fl oz (225 ml/1 cup) boiling water

2 teasp red wine vinegar

2 teasp ground cumin

1 teasp salt

20 grinds black pepper

1 pinch cayenne pepper, or 1 teasp mild chilli powder

1 bay leaf

2 rounded tbsp raisins

2 oz (50 g/½ cup) stuffed green olives, sliced

FOR THE GARNISH

2 oz (50 g/½ cup) toasted flaked or slivered almonds

1 For the meatballs, put the meat and raisins in a large bowl.

2 Purée all the remaining meatball ingredients in the food processor then add to the meat mixture and stir until thoroughly blended.

3 Shape into ovals each about 2 inches (5 cm) long, and chill.

4 Meanwhile prepare the sauce. In a large, deep, lidded frying pan, sauté the onion in the oil, covering the pan, until soft and golden – about 5 minutes.

5 Uncover and add the pepper and garlic, then sauté uncovered for a further 3–4 minutes before adding all the remaining ingredients (except the olives). Stir well and bring to the boil.

6 Add the meatballs, cover and simmer for 45 minutes, turning once.

TO SERVE

Stir in the olives and sprinkle with the toasted almonds.

SUGGESTED ACCOMPANIMENT

Rice or pasta.

POULTRY

Chicken Breasts in a Citrus and Port Wine Glaze

SERVES 6–8

Keeps 3 days under refrigeration

There is no need to spend time frying the breasts – their juices are protected by a coating of egg and breadcrumbs before they are cooked in the fruited sauce. They are equally delicious hot or cold.

6–8 part-boned chicken breasts, 6–7 oz (175–200 g) each, skinned

salt and ground pepper

2 eggs, beaten

6–7 oz (175–200 g/1½ cups) dried coating breadcrumbs

FOR THE GLAZE
1 × 12 oz (350 g) jar best-quality redcurrant jelly

4 fl oz (125 ml/½ cup) fruity red wine

5 fl oz (150 ml/⅔ cup) orange juice

grated rind of 1 orange or large mineola

3 tbsp port or port-type wine

FOR THE GARNISH
sections of orange or mineola

Preheat the oven to Gas 7 (425°F, 220°C).

1 Put all the ingredients for the glaze into a medium saucepan and simmer uncovered for 10 minutes to concentrate the flavour.

2 Season the chicken breasts lightly with salt and pepper, then brush with the beaten egg and roll in the crumbs. Arrange in a roasting tin large enough to hold them side by side.

3 Pour over half the glaze and cook for 15 minutes then pour over the remaining glaze and cook for a further 20 minutes, basting twice. If necessary, put under a hot grill for 2–3 minutes so that the surface of the chicken is beautifully glazed.

SUGGESTED ACCOMPANIMENTS

When hot Lemon Bulgur Timbales (see page 78) or Sesame Roast Baby New Potatoes (see page 82).

When at room temperature A Salad of Sugar Snap Peas and Roasted Peppers with Cashews in a Basil Vinaigrette (see page 91).

Chicken in the Spanish Style with a Wine and Almond Sauce

SERVES 6–8

Keeps 2 days under refrigeration. Freeze 3 months

This classic Spanish dish dates from medieval times when almond 'flour' was used as a thickener instead of the coarse wheat flour generally available. The two-stage cooking makes it ideal for a dinner party.

6–8 chicken breast portions on the bone, rib cage trimmed, then skinned

2 oz (50 g/½ cup) flour

1 teasp salt

15 grinds black pepper

3 tbsp extra virgin olive oil

1 large (8 oz/225 g) onion, finely chopped

1 bay leaf

10 fl oz (275 ml/1¼ cups) dry but fruity white wine

10 fl oz (275 ml/1¼ cups) hot water with ⅔ chicken stock cube

2½ oz (65 g/½ cup) ground almonds

2 hard-boiled egg yolks

2 cloves garlic, crushed

a few threads (or ¼ teasp powdered) saffron or turmeric

FOR THE GARNISH
2 oz (50 g/½ cup) slivered almonds, toasted

1 hard-boiled egg, grated and mixed with 1 tbsp chopped parsley

1 Put the flour, salt and pepper into a plastic bag and shake the breasts in it, one at a time, until evenly coated.

2 Fry the breasts in the hot oil until a rich golden brown on both sides. Drain and transfer to a baking tin large enough to hold them in one layer.

3 To make the sauce, sauté the onion in the same oil, covering the pan, until a rich golden brown and beginning to 'melt'. Add the bay leaf and wine and bubble for 3 minutes to concentrate the flavour, then add the stock, cover and leave to simmer gently.

4 Put the ground almonds, hard-boiled egg yolks, garlic and saffron or turmeric in the bowl of the food processor. Process until paste-like, then add a cupful of the simmering sauce through the feed tube. Process until a smooth creamy mixture is formed.

5 Return to the pan, stir well and leave to cool until just before serving. This can all be done earlier in the day.

Preheat the oven to Gas 5 (375°F, 190°C).

6 To complete the cooking, bake the chicken for 20 minutes. Reheat the sauce gently until simmering, then discard the bay leaf.

TO SERVE

Arrange the chicken breasts on a heated platter and coat with the hot sauce. Scatter with the toasted almonds and the egg and parsley mixture.

SUGGESTED ACCOMPANIMENTS

Boiled new potatoes or Simla Rice (see page 88).

Baked Breasts of Chicken with a Meaux Mustard and Tarragon Wine Sauce

SERVES 6

Keeps 3 days under refrigeration

The chicken breasts are baked to crispness in a highly seasoned crumb coating which, together with the lemon marinade, also keeps their flesh succulent. Both the chicken and the sauce can be prepared well in advance.

6 × 4–5 oz (125–150 g) chicken breasts, skinned and boned

3 tbsp fresh lemon juice

a little sunflower oil

FOR THE COATING
1½ tbsp Meaux mustard

3 tbsp extra virgin olive oil

15 g (½ oz) pack tarragon, finely snipped (save half for the sauce)

4 oz (125 g/1 cup) browned dried breadcrumbs

grated rind of 1 lemon

2 oz (50 g/½ cup) white sesame seeds

1 teasp salt

20 grinds black pepper

FOR THE SAUCE
2 shallots, or the bulbs of 4 large spring onions, finely chopped

2 tbsp sunflower oil

3 tbsp medium sherry

5 fl oz (150 ml/⅔ cup) white wine or vermouth

5 fl oz (150 ml/⅔ cup) hot water with ⅓ chicken stock cube

1 teasp Meaux mustard

2 teasp cornflour mixed with a little water or stock

a good pinch each of ground nutmeg and white pepper

1 egg yolk

the remainder of the tarragon (save 6 sprigs for garnish)

1 At least an hour in advance (longer will do no harm), put the lemon juice in a shallow dish and lay the breasts in it, turning them once or twice during the marinating time.

Preheat the oven to Gas 7 (425°F, 220°C).

2 For the coating, mix together the mustard, oil and tarragon in a bowl. In a shallow dish mix together the browned crumbs, lemon rind, sesame seeds and seasonings.

3 Lightly oil a baking tray. Brush the chicken breasts evenly with the mustard and oil mixture and then pat on the crumb mixture.

4 Bake the breasts for 20 minutes until golden and crisp.

5 The sauce can be done at any convenient time beforehand. Sauté the finely chopped shallots or spring onions in the oil until softened and golden then add

2 tbsp of the sherry and bubble until it has almost evaporated. Add the white wine and the stock and simmer gently (uncovered) for 5 minutes then stir in the mustard, the cornflour mixture and the seasonings. Simmer for 3 minutes then whisk in the remaining tbsp of sherry, the egg yolk and the tarragon.

TO SERVE
Spoon a swirl of sauce on each dinner plate and top it with a chicken breast; garnish with a sprig of tarragon.

SUGGESTED ACCOMPANIMENTS
Boiled new potatoes with chopped parsley, and A Stir-Fry of Baby Vegetables (see page 89).

— *Cook's Tip* —
WINE AS AN INGREDIENT
A glass or two of wine added to the cooking pot can transform a mundane casserole into a memorable dish. However it's not the alcohol that does the trick – that's quickly driven off in the cooking. Rather it's the flavour of the grapes from which the wine was made that works the magic. We generally simmer it uncovered to concentrate this flavour before completing the cooking in a covered dish.

For this job, a vintage has no more to offer than a cheap and cheerful *vin de pays* with plenty of fruit in it. Many of these useful if unremarkable wines are now sold by the 250 ml (9 fl oz) can which holds two generous glasses. You can go down another road and buy a litre bottle of a good drinking wine – then use some of it to cook with, or use the remains of the bottle left over from a previous occasion which you've vacuum sealed to conserve its flavour (you can buy a handy gadget to do this). In any event, the words 'full' or 'fruity' on the label will tell you that a particular wine is likely to have flavour potential in the pot.

Fragrant Roasted Poussins with a Pine Kernel Sauce

SERVES 4

For 6–8 servings use half as much again of the sauce

This is a dish of poussins or chicken breasts in a magnificent sauce-cum-glaze. The use of the whole spices gives the dish an intensity of flavour you can't achieve with ready-ground ones.

3½ oz (100g/1 cup) pine kernels

2 teasp ground fennel

6 teasp ground coriander

1 teasp ground cardamom

1 good pinch cayenne pepper

1 teasp saffron threads (optional)

2 large poussins or grilling chickens, split, or 4 chicken breasts on the bone

2 fl oz (50 ml/¼ cup) sunflower oil

1 medium onion, finely chopped

2 cloves garlic, finely chopped

1½ inch (3.75 cm) piece peeled ginger, finely chopped

2 tbsp tomato purée

1 teasp salt

8 fl oz (225 ml/1 cup) hot water with ½ chicken stock cube

1 red and 1 yellow pepper, seeded and cut into 1 inch (2.5 cm) pieces

1 In a small frying pan, dry-fry 3 tbsp of the pine kernels until golden brown, then reserve for garnish.

2 Crush the remainder of the pine kernels to a powder in a mortar, or using the end of a rolling pin, and mix with the spices. Set aside.

3 In a large sauté pan, brown the well-dried birds or joints in 1 tbsp of the oil until golden brown then lift out on to a plate.

4 Add the remaining oil and the chopped onion to the sauté pan and cook until golden, stirring, then add the garlic and ginger and cook for 2 minutes. Add the spice-nut mixture and cook for 1 minute. Stir in the tomato purée, salt and stock.

5 Add the birds or joints to the pan, spoon the sauce over them and bring to the boil, then reduce the heat until the liquid is simmering. Cover and cook over very gentle heat, basting often, until the birds are fork tender – about 30 minutes. Alternatively, cook for 40 minutes in the oven preheated to Gas 2 (300°F, 150°C).

6 Add the peppers and cook for 5 minutes until just tender. Taste and re-season.

TO SERVE

Arrange the poussins or chicken on a heated platter, surround with the peppers, spoon over the sauce and garnish with the reserved pine kernels.

SUGGESTED ACCOMPANIMENT

Boiled Basmati rice flavoured with half a dozen whole cardamom pods.

Devilled Poussins

SERVES 4

Leftovers keep 3 days under refrigeration

Chicken breasts on the bone can also be treated in the same way. Despite their individual intensity of flavour, all the seasonings blend together harmoniously.

4 poussins

4 tbsp sunflower oil

FOR THE 'DEVIL' MIXTURE
1 tbsp salt

1 tbsp sugar

1 teasp ground black pepper

2 teasp ground ginger

2 teasp dry mustard

2 teasp medium-strength curry powder

FOR THE GLAZE
4 tbsp peach chutney

2 tbsp Worcestershire sauce

2 tbsp light soy sauce

4 tbsp Chinese-style fruit sauce (gooseberry, plum or damson)

1 tbsp *sweet* chilli sauce

5 fl oz (150 ml/⅔ cup) hot water with ⅓ chicken stock cube

FOR THE GARNISH
4 small sprigs watercress

1 Split the poussins in half and cut away the back and rib bones.

2 Mix the 'devil' ingredients together and rub well into the surface of the birds. Leave for at least 1 hour in an ovenproof dish or on a baking tray with shallow sides.

Preheat the oven to Gas 6 (400°F, 200°C).

3 Brush the poussins with most of the oil and bake in the oven for 30 minutes.

4 To make the glaze, mix all the sauces together with any remaining oil, heat gently (1½ minutes on 100% in the microwave), then spoon over the poussins.

5 Continue to cook under a preheated grill for 4–5 minutes, basting with the glaze until the skin is dark golden brown and crisp. Arrange in serving dish.

6 Dilute the glaze left in the dish with the 5 fl oz (150 ml/⅔ cup) stock and spoon around the poussins.

TO SERVE

Garnish with watercress.

SUGGESTED ACCOMPANIMENT

Simla Rice (see page 88).

Grilled Chicken Breasts on a Salad of Fresh Mango and Crisp Leaves

SERVES 6

Leftover cooked chicken keeps 3 days under refrigeration.

A dish from the modern Californian cuisine – rich in flavour but simple in execution. The breasts are best cooked not more than 30 minutes before serving.

6 × 5 oz (150 g) chicken breast fillets, unskinned and lightly salted

FOR THE TOPPING
½ 12 oz (360 g) jar mango chutney (about 4 rounded tbsp)

2 teasp garlic purée or 2 cloves garlic, crushed

1 tbsp light soy sauce

1 tbsp lemon juice

1 tbsp brown sugar

3 teasp minced ginger or 1 inch (2.5 cm) piece peeled fresh ginger, finely chopped

FOR THE DRESSING
2 tbsp hazelnut or walnut oil

1½ tbsp balsamic (or cider) vinegar

4 tbsp extra virgin oil

½ teasp salt

10 grinds black pepper

1 pinch sugar

1 pinch dry mustard

FOR THE SALAD
2 × 4 oz (125 g) packs Continental-style salad leaves

1 ripe mango, peeled then sliced or diced

FOR THE GARNISH
3 tbsp honey-roasted cashews

1 Mix together all the ingredients for the topping then spread on the chicken breasts. Place in a foil-lined grill pan, and leave at room temperature for 30 minutes.

2 Preheat the grill then arrange the grill pan 4 inches (10 cm) away from the heat. Grill the chicken for 10 minutes, basting three or four times, then nick one breast to make sure no pinkness remains. Alternatively the breasts can be roasted in the oven preheated to Gas 7 (425°F, 220°C) for 25–30 minutes, basting three or four times. Leave to cool for at least 30 minutes.

3 Shake all the dressing ingredients together in a screw-top jar until thickened – about 1 minute.

4 Turn the salad leaves and the mango sections into a large bowl and toss with just enough of the dressing to coat them until they are glistening.

TO SERVE
Turn the salad on to a platter, and arrange the chicken breasts, sliced but left with the base intact, on top. Scatter with the nuts.

Roast Duck with a Ginger Glaze, and an Apple and Drambuie Sauce

S E R V E S   8

Leftover duck keeps 3 days, sauce 4 days, under refrigeration

This is our host/hostess-friendly way of handling duck to avoid wrestling with the carving just before serving.

2 × 5–5½ lb (2.25–2.5 kg) ducks, excess fat removed

salt

1 orange, quartered

1 lemon, quartered

FOR THE SAUCE
1½ lb (675 g) Bramley cooking apples, peeled, cored and thinly sliced

2 oz (50 g/¼ cup) brown sugar

2 tbsp lime juice

1 teasp grated fresh ginger, or
1 teasp ginger purée

5 tbsp Drambuie liqueur

8 grinds black pepper

FOR THE GLAZE
4 rounded tbsp ginger conserve

Preheat the oven to Gas 4 (350°F, 180°C).

1 *To roast the ducks – stage 1:* On the morning of the day you intend to serve the ducks, dry them thoroughly inside and out with paper towels, then wrap in more towels and leave for 30 minutes.

2 Remove the towels, prick the ducks all over with a sharp fork, and arrange side by side on a rack over a roasting tin.

3 Sprinkle with salt, and put two pieces of orange and two of lemon inside each duck. Roast for 2½ hours, or until the juices run clear when a leg is pierced. Pour off the fat.

4 While the ducks are roasting, make the sauce. Put the prepared apples, sugar and lime juice into a covered pan or microwave-safe casserole. Simmer on top of the stove until pulpy, or cook on 100% power in the microwave for 6 minutes. Turn the mixture into a bowl and whisk in all the remaining ingredients until smooth.

5 Carve the cooled ducks. Halve them, cut out the backbone, then divide in four by cutting diagonally between breast and leg so everyone gets some breast. Arrange the portions in the cleaned roasting tin. At this stage, the ducks can be refrigerated.

6 *To roast the ducks – stage 2:* About 1½ hours before serving, remove the duck portions from the refrigerator and leave to stand for 1 hour. Preheat the oven to Gas 7 (425°F, 220°C).

7 Spread with ginger conserve and roast for 25 minutes until crisp.

T O   S E R V E

Reheat the sauce and serve with the glazed duck portions.

VEGETARIAN

Three-Cheese Feuilleton

SERVES 6–8

This should be served freshly baked

A spongy cheese filling is enclosed in light-as-air crisp layers of puff pastry. The blue cheese adds a pungent note.

14–16 oz (400–450 g) puff pastry, in two equal pieces

FOR THE FILLING
6 oz (175 g/1½ cups) Cheddar cheese, grated

8 oz (225 g/1 cup) curd (medium-fat) cheese

1 oz (25 g/¼ cup) blue cheese, crumbled

1 egg, beaten

½ teasp paprika pepper

1 tbsp chopped fresh parsley or coriander, or 1 teasp freeze-dried coriander

1 tbsp fresh chives, snipped, or 1 teasp freeze-dried

FOR THE GLAZE
1 egg yolk mixed with 1 tbsp water

2 tbsp sesame seeds

1 For the filling, put the cheeses into a bowl. Stir in the egg, paprika and herbs.

2 Roll each half of the pastry into a rectangle of 15 × 6 inches (37.5 × 15 cm). The one to be used for the top should be *slightly* larger to allow for the filling. Place the lower piece of pastry on an ungreased tray (or one lined with silicone paper), and spoon the filling on top, leaving a 1 inch (2.5 cm) border clear all the way round.

3 Fold the top piece of pastry in two lengthways and make six 1 inch (2.5 cm) wide cuts down the middle (to allow steam to escape). Moisten the border on the lower piece of pastry with cold water, then lay the top piece in position, sealing the edges well together and flaking them with the back of a knife. Chill until ready to bake (the feuilleton can now be refrigerated for up to 6 hours).

4 Preheat the oven to Gas 8 (450°F, 230°C). Paint the egg glaze all over the feuilleton. Bake for 15 minutes then re-glaze and scatter with the sesame seeds. Turn the oven down to Gas 6 (400°F, 200°C) and bake for a further 15–20 minutes. The feuilleton should be well risen, crisp to the touch and richly browned.

TO SERVE
Allow to cool for 5–10 minutes before serving in slices with one or two salads.

SUGGESTED ACCOMPANIMENTS
French bread and a tomato salad, or Herbed Tomato Chutney (see page 95).

A Feuilleton of Woodland Mushrooms and Pine Kernels

SERVES 6–8

Serve the same day

The rich mushroom filling has an almost 'meaty' flavour, making this a particularly satisfying vegetarian dish. The shiny, chestnut-coloured glaze makes for a stunning presentation on the table.

14–16 oz (400–450 g) puff pastry in two equal pieces

FOR THE FILLING
1 fat clove garlic, halved

2 tbsp extra virgin olive oil

4 shallots, finely chopped

1½ lb (675 g/7½ cups) mixed mushrooms (Paris brown, oyster, shiitake, white), thinly sliced

6 shakes ground nutmeg

1 teasp salt

20 grinds black pepper

3 fl oz (75 ml/⅓ cup) Amontillado (medium dry) sherry

2 rounded tbsp coarsely chopped fresh parsley

2 oz (50 g/½ cup) toasted pine kernels

FOR THE GLAZE
1 egg yolk plus 2 teasp cold water

1 To start the filling, in a large sauté pan, cook the halves of garlic in the oil until golden then discard them – this flavours the oil. In the same oil sauté the shallots until golden then add the mushrooms and cook briskly, tossing them in the pan, until they are beginning to brown. Sprinkle with the seasonings then pour in the sherry and cook until the moisture has almost evaporated. Stir in the parsley and pine kernels. Taste and re-season if necessary, then leave to cool.

2 Roll and fill as for the Three-Cheese Feuilleton (see page 72).
Preheat the oven to Gas 8 (450°F, 230°C).

3 Glaze the top of the feuilleton with the egg and water. Bake the feuilleton for 15 minutes then open the oven and re-glaze. Turn the oven down to Gas 6 (400°F, 200°C), and bake for a further 15 minutes until a rich brown.

TO SERVE
Allow to cool for 5–10 minutes before serving in slices with one or two salads.

SUGGESTED ACCOMPANIMENTS
Dressed green salad and a Salad of Artichoke Hearts with a Lemon and Tarragon Dressing (see page 92).

Asparagus Strudel with Garden Herbs

SERVES 6–8: MAKES 2 STRUDELS

Serve freshly baked

A perfect strudel for early summer, packed with a bouquet of fresh herbs and young vegetables.

1 × 14 oz (140 g) packet filo pastry (8 sheets are required)

4 oz (125 g/½ cup) butter, melted

FOR THE FILLING
2 × 9 oz (250 g) packs frozen asparagus, thawed

2 oz (50 g/¼ cup) butter

the white part of 2 young leeks, thinly sliced

1 shallot or 3 spring onion bulbs, finely chopped

8 oz (225 g) Gruyère or Jarlsberg cheese, finely grated

3 eggs, beaten

2 tbsp each of chopped fresh mint, fresh parsley, fresh dill and fresh snipped chives

1 teasp salt

20 grinds black pepper

½ teasp paprika pepper

1 pinch cayenne pepper

1½ tbsp fresh lemon juice

2 oz (50 g/½ cup) flaked almonds, toasted

FOR SPRINKLING
1 tbsp each of sesame seeds and poppy seeds

1 For the filling, lay the defrosted asparagus on a double thickness of paper towels to remove excess moisture, then cut in 1 inch (2.5 cm) lengths. Place in a large bowl.

2 Melt the butter and sauté the leeks and shallots (or spring onions) until soft and transparent, then add to the asparagus together with all the other filling ingredients. Mix gently but thoroughly and adjust the seasoning if necessary. Preheat the oven to Gas 5 (375°F, 190°C).

3 To assemble each strudel, proceed as follows. Assemble them *separately*. Take four sheets from the packet and lay one on top of each other, brushing each one in turn with a thin layer of melted butter.

4 Arrange half the asparagus mixture across the lower edge of the pastry layer in a long strip 3 inches (7.5 cm) wide, leaving 3 inches (7.5 cm) clear on the bottom edge and 1 inch (2.5 cm) on either side. Turn in the sides to enclose the filling then roll up into a strudel and arrange on a greased tray, join down. Cut through the top layer of pastry at 2 inch (5 cm) intervals.

5 Repeat with another four sheets of pastry and the remaining filling.

6 Brush the tops and sides of each strudel with a thin layer of butter and scatter with the mixed seeds.

7 Bake for 30–35 minutes until a rich golden brown. (The strudels may be refrigerated for up to 2 hours before baking.)

TO SERVE
Allow the strudels to cool for 10 minutes then slice and serve.

SUGGESTED ACCOMPANIMENTS
Chilled Cacik (see page 36), granary rolls and a crisp green salad with garlic croûtons.

— *Cook's Tip* —
GRATING IN THE FOOD PROCESSOR
Before you attempt to grate any food with a high fat content, such as cheese or marzipan, in the food processor, it's vital to chill it well. We know because we didn't and ended up with a gummed-up machine and a pound of gunge. It's the high-speed action of the machine which in turn generates heat that is the problem. To overcome it, cut the food to a size that will fit the tube then freeze the pieces for 30 minutes. It will then pass through the grating attachment like a dream — and faster than you can say 'cheese'!

Aubergine, Garlic and Sun-Dried Tomato Tart

SERVES 6–8

Raw pastry case keeps 1 day under refrigeration. Freezes 3 months. Leftover tart keeps 2 days under refrigeration

All the flavours of the Mediterranean in one glorious tart.

1 recipe Brown Herb Pastry (see page 125), or 12 oz (350 g) ready-to-use shortcrust pastry

FOR THE FILLING
1 fat head of garlic

olive oil drained from sun-dried tomatoes (and additional extra virgin olive oil if necessary)

1 lb (450 g) unpeeled aubergines, sliced ¾ inch (2 cm) thick on the diagonal

salt and ground black pepper

1 tbsp chopped fresh marjoram or chives

3 large eggs

5 fl oz (150 ml/⅔ cup) single cream

7 fl oz (200 ml/⅞ cup) crème fraîche

4 oz (125 g) Gruyère cheese, thinly sliced

4 oz (125 g/½ cup) sun-dried tomatoes packed in oil, drained and thinly sliced

1 Line an 11–12 inch (27.5–30 cm) loose-bottomed flan tin with the chilled pastry rolled ⅛ inch (3 mm) thick. Freeze while you prepare the filling. Preheat the oven to Gas 6 (400°F, 200°C).

2 Brush the head of garlic with a little oil and roast it on a baking sheet until soft, about 30 minutes. When the garlic has cooled, cut the top off the bulb and squeeze the cloves out of their skins. Set aside half the cloves (whole) for the tart and mash the remaining cloves for the savoury custard.

3 The aubergine can be roasted in the same oven and at the same time as the garlic. Brush both sides of the slices with the oil, lay them on a baking sheet and sprinkle with salt and pepper. Roast until the slices are soft, about 15 minutes. Cool, cut each slice into two or three strips, and toss with the fresh herbs. Reduce the oven temperature to Gas 5 (375°F, 190°C).

4 Beat the eggs to blend in a bowl then whisk in the mashed roasted garlic, followed by the creams, and some salt and pepper.

5 Arrange the sliced cheese on the bottom of the pastry-lined tart tin. Lay the aubergine strips on the cheese, followed by the roasted garlic cloves and sun-dried tomatoes. Pour the custard over the vegetables and bake for about 30–35 minutes, until the custard sets and turns golden. Serve warm or at room temperature.

SUGGESTED ACCOMPANIMENT

An Orange, Watercress and Toasted Sunflower Seed Salad (see page 25).

Accompaniments

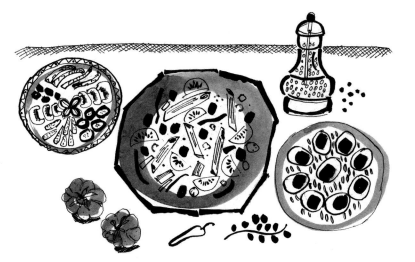

We've raided the repertoires of cooks from many countries to ring the changes on the traditional accompaniments of potatoes and two veg. Grains, pasta and rice are all very tasty, good-tempered alternatives to potatoes which can be partnered with the new varieties of miniature vegetables that only need a quick stir-fry before they're brought to the table. There is, however, still something very comforting about the potato so we've sauced it, creamed it, sautéed it, and roasted it with herbs or seeds to give it an exciting new image.

For good measure, we've also included some ideas for cooked vegetables in salads – very useful if you're single-handed in the kitchen. In this section you'll also find two stunning relishes – one sweet and sour, the other spicy – to accompany a main dish.

Lemon Bulgur Timbales
SERVES 6–8
Cooked bulgur keeps under refrigeration for 3 days. Freeze 3 months

Lighter on the tongue than rice, bulgur (cracked wheat) fulfils a similar role as an accompaniment. It is also sold as cracked wheat, pourgouri or bourghoul and is generally sold par-cooked (also called 'parched') – the type we always use. Timbales add a note of refinement to a dinner party main course, but for simpler service put the bulgur into a covered oven-to-table dish so it can be reheated when required (either in a moderate oven or a microwave), until piping hot.

1 large bunch spring onions, trimmed + 4 inches (10 cm) of the green, finely sliced

2 oz (50 g/¼ cup) butter or margarine

12 oz (350 g/2 cups) bulgur (cracked wheat)

finely grated rind of 1 large lemon

1½ pints (850 ml/3¾ cups) hot water with 2 chicken or vegetable stock cubes

salt and freshly ground black pepper

FOR THE GARNISH
1 tbsp coarsely snipped chives

1 In an 8 inch (20 cm) saucepan or sauté pan, cook the spring onions over moderate heat in the fat, stirring until softened, then add the bulgur and the lemon rind and cook the mixture, stirring, for 1 minute.

2 Add the stock, bring to the boil, cover, and simmer the mixture for 10 minutes, or until the liquid is absorbed.

3 Fluff up with a fork then let it stand, covered but off the heat, for 5 minutes. Taste and season if necessary with a little salt and pepper. (It may be refrigerated or frozen at this point.)

TO SERVE
Using an oiled 5 fl oz (150 ml) timbale mould and, forming one timbale at a time, pack the bulgur mixture into the mould and invert it on dinner plates. Garnish with a few snipped chives.

Curried Couscous and Red Pepper Timbales

Serves 6

Keeps 3 days under refrigeration

An excellent dish to serve with roast or grilled meat or poultry. For a dinner party it looks very pretty turned out of a timbale mould, but for a less formal meal it can be served from the dish.

1 medium (5 oz/150 g) onion, finely chopped

2 tbsp butter or margarine

1½ tbsp mild curry powder

1 small green pepper, finely diced

1 small red pepper, finely diced

5 fl oz (150 ml/⅔ cup) hot water with ½ chicken or vegetable stock cube

4 oz (125 g/¾ cup) couscous

¼ teasp salt

10 grinds black pepper

1 In a frying pan sauté the onion in the fat over moderate heat, stirring until it is softened.

2 Add the curry powder and cook for 30 seconds, then add the peppers and cook, stirring for a further minute.

3 Add the stock, bring to the boil and stir in the couscous.

4 Let the mixture stand, covered, off the heat, for 5 minutes, season it with the salt and pepper and fluff with a fork.

To serve

Either pack each serving into a timbale mould and unmould on a platter or individual plate, or cook ahead then transfer to a microwave-safe dish, cover and reheat on 100% power for 3 minutes.

Bulgur and Vermicelli Pilaff

SERVES 6–7

Keeps 3 days under refrigeration. Freeze for 3 months

A light yet satisfying accompaniment to any meat or poultry. Particularly good to serve with a braised dish. The dish reheats well, either in a moderate oven or more conveniently in the microwave (3 minutes in a covered dish on 100% power).

1 large onion (8 oz/225 g), finely chopped

3 tbsp sunflower oil

3 oz (75 g/½ cup) vermicelli, broken into short lengths

9 oz (250 g/1½ cups) bulgur (cracked wheat)

1 teasp salt

20 grinds black pepper

approx. 22 fl oz (625 ml/2¾ cups) hot water with 1½ chicken stock cubes

TO DRIZZLE
2 teasp roasted sesame oil

1 Sauté the onion in the oil until soft and golden brown – about 5 minutes.

2 Add the vermicelli, then stir around in the onion for a further 3 minutes.

3 Add the bulgur, season, and continue to cook for a further 3 or 4 minutes.

4 Finally add enough of the hot stock barely to cover the mixture. Cover and simmer until the stock has been absorbed – about 10 minutes.

5 Taste to ensure the bulgur is tender. Turn off the heat, cover the pan with a tea towel under the lid, and stand for 10 minutes.

TO SERVE

Turn into a hot dish and drizzle with the sesame oil.

— Cook's Tip —
BULGUR AND THE MICROWAVE

The microwave doesn't cook this nutty-flavoured grain any quicker than the stove, but it does cook it right in the serving dish – and without any attention. This simple dish provides the perfect foil to any highly flavoured chicken or meat casserole.

To cook 6 generous portions: put 9 oz (50 g/1½ cups) bulgur, 3 teasp minced dried onion, and 1¼ pints (725 ml/3 cups) boiling chicken or vegetable stock into a deep lidded casserole. Stir in 1 tbsp any oil, cover and cook on 100% power for 6 minutes or until bubbling. Turn down to 50% power for a further 4 minutes, then leave to stand, covered, for 5 minutes. Fluff up with a fork and serve.

Bulgur and Pine Kernel Pilaff

SERVES 6–8

Keeps 2 days under refrigeration. Freeze 3 months

A very convenient dish which reheats well in the microwave – allow 3 minutes in a covered dish at 100% power or until piping hot. Allow 20 minutes in a moderate oven, Gas 4 (350°F, 180°C). It's equally delicious served cold as a variation on the more usual tabbouleh.

1 large (8 oz/225 g) onion, finely chopped	1½ pints (850 ml/3¾ cups) hot water with 2 chicken stock cubes
3 tbsp sunflower oil, or 2 oz (50 g/¼ cup) butter	salt and freshly ground black pepper
12 oz (350 g/2 cups) bulgur (cracked wheat)	2 oz (50 g/¼ cup) toasted pine kernels
2 teasp freshly grated orange rind	2 oz (50 g/¼ cup) chopped parsley
6 tbsp raisins	1 small bunch spring onions, finely sliced

1 In an 8–9 inch (20–22.5 cm) saucepan, sauté the onion in the oil or butter over moderate heat, stirring until it is softened.

2 Stir in the bulgur and the orange rind and cook the mixture, stirring, for 1 minute.

3 Add the raisins and the stock, bring the liquid to the boil and cook, covered, over low heat for 10 minutes or until the liquid is absorbed. Fluff the pilaff with a fork to separate the grains and add salt and black pepper to taste.

TO SERVE

When hot   Stir in the pine kernels, parsley and spring onions.

When cold   Allow the pilaff to cool for 15 minutes before stirring in the remaining ingredients. It may be prepared up to this point 6 hours in advance and kept chilled, covered loosely, until 30 minutes before serving.

Roast Baby New Potatoes

SERVES 6–8

Serve immediately

These crisp mouthfuls have the added advantage of cooking in half the time of regular roast potatoes.

1½–2 lb (675–900 g) ready-to-cook baby new potatoes

salt and freshly ground black pepper

1½ teasp freeze-dried herbes de Provence

3 tbsp extra virgin olive oil

sea salt

1 Cover the potatoes with cold water, add 1 teasp salt, bring to the boil and cook for 8 minutes or until almost tender. Drain and dry off well (most easily with a tea towel laid over them in the pan).

Preheat the oven to Gas 7 (425°F, 220°C).

2 In a roasting tin just large enough to hold the potatoes in one layer, mix the herbs and oil together then toss the potatoes in this until well coated. Season with salt and pepper and roast for 40 minutes or until crisp and golden brown.

TO SERVE

Sprinkle lightly with sea salt and freshly ground black pepper.

Sesame Roast Baby New Potatoes

SERVES 6–8

1½–2 lb (675–900 g) baby new potatoes

salt and freshly ground black pepper

3 tbsp walnut oil

2 tbsp sesame seeds

Prepare and cook as in the above recipe, but substitute walnut oil for the olive oil and sesame seeds for the herbs.

OPPOSITE

Fragrant Roasted Poussins with Pine Kernel Sauce (page 68) *served with* *A Stir-Fry of Baby Vegetables* (page 89)

Creamed Potatoes in the Greek Style

SERVES 6–8

Leftovers keep 1 day under refrigeration

A dish of creamy mashed potatoes can be the stuff of dreams. The herbs can only add to what is already perfection. Be sure to whisk in only *hot* liquid as this preserves the fluffy texture.

2½ lb (1.1 kg) Maris Piper or other good boiling potatoes (weight when peeled)

salt

5 fl oz (150 ml/⅔ cup) 'half and half' milk and single cream, warmed

1 oz (25 g/2 tbsp) butter

½ teasp white pepper

½ teasp ground nutmeg

1 beaten egg

1 oz (25 g/4 tbsp) each of fresh chopped dill and parsley

FOR THE TOPPING
a thick layer of grated Cheddar cheese (about 4 oz/125 g/ 1¼ cups)

1 Cook the peeled and quartered potatoes in a covered pan of boiling water seasoned with 1 teasp salt until tender when pierced with a slim pointed knife – about 15 minutes. Drain the water off then return the pan to the stove and shake over gentle heat until all the surface moisture has evaporated from the potatoes.

2 Pour the half and half milk and cream down the side of the pan and when it starts to steam, add the butter, pepper, nutmeg and salt to taste.

3 Whisk the potatoes over the lowest heat (most easily with a hand-held electric whisk) until they lighten in colour and look creamy in texture. Whisk in the egg. Stir in the herbs.

4 Pile into a gratin dish, smooth level then scatter with the cheese and dot with the butter.

TO SERVE AT ONCE
Grill until golden brown and crunchy on top. Serve from the dish.

TO REHEAT AND SERVE
Either reheat in the oven preheated to Gas 6 (400°F, 200°C) for 15 minutes, or reheat in the microwave for 3 minutes on 100% power until very hot to the touch then brown under the grill as before. Serve from the dish.

OPPOSITE

Aubergine, Garlic and Sun-Dried Tomato Tart (page 76) *served with Orange, Watercress and Toasted Sunflower Seed Salad* (page 25)

Sauté of Potatoes with Pistachios

S E R V E S   8

Cooked potatoes will keep for 2 days under refrigeration

2½–3 lb (1.1–1.4 kg) baking potatoes, peeled and cut in little cubes

2 cloves garlic, crushed

1 good pinch salt

3 oz (75 g/⅓ cup) butter or margarine, melted

2 oz (50 g/½ cup) natural shelled pistachios, chopped

Preheat the oven to Gas 5 (375°F, 190°C), though if more convenient it can be slightly lower or higher and the cooking time adjusted accordingly.

1 Mix together the potatoes, garlic, salt, fat, and pistachios. Arrange in a shallow baking dish and cover with foil.

2 Bake for 20 minutes, then open the foil and stir the potatoes well. Bake for a further 20 minutes, still covered.

3 Remove the foil and bake for a further 15 minutes until golden brown.

Note   If more convenient the potatoes can be cooked to stage 2 then refrigerated, covered, for up to 24 hours. Shortly before serving remove the foil as directed in stage 3 then bake as before for a further 20 minutes until crisp and golden brown.

Pommes Lyonnaise

S E R V E S   6 – 8

Cooked vegetables keep 2 days under refrigeration, ready for final browning

This dish may score high in calories – but the flavour and the crunch surely make them well spent. This method cuts out tedious pan-watching by crisping the vegetables in the oven instead.

3 lb (1.4 kg) roasting potatoes (Edwards, Maris Piper)

1 teasp salt

3 oz (75 g/⅓ cup) butter or margarine, plus 3 tbsp sunflower oil, or 6 tbsp sunflower oil

1 large (8 oz/225 g) onion, finely chopped or thinly sliced

sea salt and freshly ground black pepper

FOR THE GARNISH
1 tbsp chopped parsley

I Scrub the potatoes if necessary then cook them whole in their skins, covered with boiling salted water, until tender – 25–40 minutes (test with the point of a sharp knife). Drain off the water then leave them in the pan, covered with kitchen paper or tea towel to dry off. Leave until they are cool enough to handle, then skin and cut in ½ inch (1.25 cm) cubes.

2 Heat the chosen fat(s) in a frying pan until a comfortable warmth can be felt on the hand held 2 inches (5 cm) above it.

3 Add the onion and cook gently until soft and golden – about 10 minutes. Remove to an oven tray wide enough to hold the onions and the potatoes in one layer – a large roulade tin is ideal.

4 Put the potatoes in the frying pan and cook, shaking frequently, until they are a light golden colour – they should slowly absorb the fat rather than fry in it. Turn into the tin and mix well with the onions. Leave until an hour before serving. Preheat the oven to Gas 7 (425°F, 220°C).

5 Put the tin with the potatoes and onions into the oven and cook for 1 hour, until crisp and golden, shaking them occasionally. The potatoes can then be kept hot for up to 20 minutes in a moderate oven until required.

To serve

Turn into a serving dish, season with a few grinds of sea salt and black pepper and sprinkle with the parsley.

Gratin of Potatoes à la Dauphinoise

SERVES 6–8

Leftovers keep 2 days under refrigeration. Do not freeze

This glorious dish is surprisingly good tempered – hence its popularity in so many restaurants as a 'side dish'. It can be cooked either in the oven or microwave – provided the temperature permits the cream to bubble gently but never boil. When time is short, bring it to simmering in the microwave then cut half an hour off the oven cooking time.

2 lb (900 g) baking potatoes

⅛ teasp ground nutmeg

salt

10 grinds black pepper

10 fl oz (275 ml/1¼ cups) whipping cream

4 oz (125 g/1 cup) Gruyère cheese, grated

1–2 oz (25–50 g/¼–½ cup) Parmesan Cheese, grated

1 oz (25 g/2 tbsp) butter, melted + 1 teasp for greasing

Preheat the oven to Gas 4 (350°F, 180°C).

1 Peel then finely slice the potatoes (most easily in the food processor). Soak in cold water for 5 minutes, then dab dry.

2 Add the nutmeg, ½ teasp salt and the pepper to the cream, mixing well. Mix the cheeses together.

3 Lightly butter a gratin dish approximately 1½ inches (3.75 cm) deep.

4 Arrange a layer of the potatoes in overlapping rows on the bottom of the dish and season lightly with salt, then spoon over a third of the seasoned cream, a third of the mixed cheese and a splash of the melted butter.

5 Repeat twice, ending with a layer of cheese and the remaining butter.

6 Cover lightly with silicone paper and bake for 1½ hours until the potatoes are tender when pierced with a sharp knife and the top is golden brown and crusty. If the cream starts to bubble fiercely during the cooking time, turn the oven down to Gas 3 (325°F, 160°C). If the potatoes are not browning well near the end of the cooking period, remove the silicone paper.

7 To cook in the microwave, layer as above in a microwave-safe dish, cover with a lid or pierced clingfilm and cook on 100% power for 30 minutes or until tender. Leave to stand for 5 minutes, then uncover and brown under a hot grill until golden.

TO SERVE

Bring to the table in the cooking dish and let guests help themselves.

Fresh Tagliatelle with 'Hazelnut' Butter and Walnuts

S E R V E S 6 – 8

Serve immediately

In this unusual presentation of pasta, the nuts and crumbs make a delicious contrast to the silkiness of the buttered tagliatelle.

2 oz (50 g/¼ cup) + 1 oz (25 g/2 tbsp) butter

12 oz (350 g) fresh tagliatelle (noodles), boiled until tender

½ teasp sea salt

15 grinds black pepper

2 oz (50 g/½ cup) toasted walnuts, finely chopped

2 oz (50 g/½ cup) Parmesan cheese, finely grated

2 oz (50 g/½ cup) dried breadcrumbs

1 To make the 'hazelnut' butter, melt the 2 oz (50 g/¼ cup) butter in a small pan and cook over medium heat until it turns pale fawn in colour. Snatch it off the heat as it begins to colour – the hot pan will complete the process.

2 Melt the remaining butter in a large pan and add the hot noodles, tossing until they are coated and glistening, then stir in the salt, pepper, walnuts, cheese and breadcrumbs which have been thoroughly mixed together. (This may be reheated in the microwave in a covered microwave-safe dish until hot.)

T O S E R V E

Turn into a hot serving dish and pour over the 'hazelnut' butter. Serve at once.

— Cook's Tip —
R E H E A T I N G P A S T A , R I C E , B U L G U R A N D C O U S C O U S

No food looks more limp and lifeless than cold pasta, rice or grains such as bulgur or couscous; nothing can bring them back to life as easily as the microwave. The food is reheated so quickly that there is no time for any health hazard to develop and both the colour and the texture are as if they'd been freshly cooked.

To reheat **pasta**, simply place in a covered container or plastic bag and reheat.

To reheat **rice, bulgur or couscous**, lightly sprinkle the surface with water, then cover tightly. As the dish heats up this will be transformed into steam, making every grain light and fluffy again.

To work out the timing, start by microwaving for 2 minutes and progress by an extra minute at a time until the food is steaming and piping hot throughout.

Simla Rice

SERVES 6–8

Keeps 3 days under refrigeration. Freeze 6 months

This basic pilaff – with or without the turmeric – is ideal for any recipe that calls for savoury rice, whether hot or cold.

1 medium onion, finely chopped	1¼ pints (725 ml/3 cups) hot water with 2 chicken or vegetable stock cubes
2 tbsp oil	
12 oz (350 g/2 cups) long-grain Patna or Basmati rice, rinsed well in cold water and drained	2 level teasp salt
	15 grinds black pepper
	1½ teasp turmeric

I In a heavy-based pan sauté the onion in the oil for 5 minutes or until soft.

2 Add the rice and turn in the onion for 3 minutes.

3 Add the hot stock, salt, pepper and turmeric, and stir well. Bring to the boil, then cover tightly and cook for 20 minutes over a low heat either on top of the stove or in a preheated oven, Gas 4 (350°F, 180°C).

TO SERVE

Leave covered to steam for 10 minutes at the end of the cooking period then use a fork to fluff up the rice, separating the grains.

— *Cook's Tip* —

TYPES OF RICE

Basmati rice is grown in the foothills of the Himalayas and is ideal for use in Indian curries and pilaus. It belongs to a very special group of rice called 'Aromatics' which have in common a naturally occurring ingredient which is responsible for their fragrant taste and aroma. Another of these aromatics is Jasmine rice (grown in Thailand) which is much used in Far Eastern dishes, but unlike Basmati, whose grains stay separate and fluffy, it does become a little sticky after cooking. We find it an ideal variety to serve with chicken or beef casseroles or with meatballs.

However, for any Indian rice dish, we put our money on Basmati. Provided that before you cook it you give it a good rinsing under the cold tap to remove excess starch, you can't fail to end up with lovely fluffy, separate grains of rice. It takes particularly kindly to a gentle spicing, Indian style, which seems to accentuate its natural flavour.

A Stir-Fry of Baby Vegetables

S E R V E S 6 – 8

Serve immediately

This dish combines the charm of the miniature with the beguiling blend of flavours used in the stir-fry. Blanching all the vegetables early in the day concentrates the final preparation and cooking time to a brief 3 minutes.

1 lb (450 g) sugar snap peas or mangetout	*FOR THE STIR-FRYING* 1½ tbsp sunflower oil
8 oz (225 g) broccoli florets	1 large clove garlic, cut in tiny slivers
8 oz (225 g) miniature asparagus, halved lengthways	1 inch (2.5 cm) piece peeled fresh ginger, cut in tiny slivers
salt	2 teasp light soy sauce
	10 grinds black pepper

1 Early in the day, cook each kind of vegetable separately either in boiling salted water or by steaming in the microwave until barely tender. Drench with cold water to set the colour, then allow to drain thoroughly.

2 Just before serving, heat the oil with the garlic and ginger slivers in a wok or wide frying pan over high heat for 3 minutes.

3 Add all the vegetables and toss over high heat until steaming – about 3 minutes.

4 Sprinkle with the soy sauce and the pepper then mix well.

T O S E R V E

Spoon into a heated dish and serve at once.

Note The stir-frying can be completed just before guests arrive and the vegetables left in the pan then reheated just before serving. However, expect the vegetables to lose some of their crispness during the waiting period.

Parsnip and Orange Purée

SERVES 6–8

Keeps 3 days under refrigeration. Freeze leftovers 3 months

The food processor takes seconds to transform plain boiled parsnips into a smooth-as-silk purée – the perfect partner for crisp roast potatoes served with a joint or bird.

2½ lb (1.1 kg) parsnips	15 grinds black pepper
salt	1 good pinch ground nutmeg
3 tbsp walnut oil	grated rind of 1 medium orange

I Peel the parsnips and remove any woody core, then cut into even-sized chunks.

2 Cook in water seasoned with 1 teasp salt until very soft when pierced with a pointed knife, then drain and put into the food processor.

3 Add the oil, 1 teasp salt, the pepper, nutmeg and orange rind, then process until smooth – the mixture should be the consistency of creamy mashed potatoes.

TO SERVE

Turn into the serving dish and decorate with a fork or the blade of a knife. To reheat, cover and cook in the microwave on 100% power for 4 minutes, or for 20 minutes in a moderate oven, at Gas 4 (350°F, 180°C).

Parsnip and Walnut Purée

Prepare and make as in the recipe above, but omit the orange rind.

3½–4 oz (100–125 g/¾-1 cup) walnuts

Toss over medium heat in an empty non-stick frying pan until they smell toasty. Pulse in with the parsnips until they are finely chopped.

A Salad of Sugar Snap Peas and Roasted Peppers with Cashews in a Basil Vinaigrette

SERVES 6–8

Serve the same day

Canned red peppers work well in this piquant salad.

1 × 14 oz (140 g) can whole roasted red peppers, drained and cut in ¼ inch (6 mm) strips

1 lb (450 g) sugar snap peas, trimmed

3 tbsp roasted cashews

FOR THE DRESSING

1½ tbsp white wine vinegar

6 tbsp extra virgin olive oil

15 grinds black pepper

½ teasp salt

1 pinch sugar

3 tbsp snipped fresh basil leaves

1 In a screw-top jar shake together the vinegar, oil and seasonings. (Leave the basil until later.) Add the strips of red pepper and leave to marinate for several hours.

2 In a large saucepan of boiling water, blanch the peas for 1–2 minutes or until barely tender. Turn at once into a colander, drench with cold water then pat dry.

3 Drain the peppers. Whisk the fresh basil into the dressing.

TO SERVE

Arrange the peas and drained peppers decoratively on individual plates. Drizzle the dressing over the vegetables. Garnish with the nuts.

— *Cook's Tip* —

CONVENIENCE INGREDIENTS

In a trawl round the major supermarkets we've found a host of attractive 'convenience ingredients' that take much of the labour out of cooking yet don't diminish its quality in any way. Examples include fresh garlic purée in a tube, chopped fresh ginger in a jar, rice vermicelli that needs no cooking, canned tomatoes that need neither chopping nor sieving, canned red peppers that need no skinning, fresh pineapple that needs neither coring nor peeling, mixed salad greens that are ready washed, and new potatoes scraped ready for the pot.

Of course there is a price to pay when the food factory takes over from the domestic kitchen. But it may not be all that excessive when it is balanced with the time and effort that can be saved.

A Salad of Artichoke Hearts with a Lemon and Tarragon Dressing

SERVES 6–8

Keeps 2 days under refrigeration

The nutty if rather bland flavour of the artichokes is emphasised by the refreshing dressing with its background of olive and nut oils. A fine accompaniment for any savoury pastry.

2 × 14 oz (140 g) cans artichoke hearts or bottoms, well drained and sliced ½ inch (1.25 cm) thick

FOR THE DRESSING
finely grated rind of 1 fine lemon

4 tbsp lemon juice

1 tbsp sherry vinegar or wine vinegar

2 fat cloves garlic, finely chopped

1 teasp salt

20 grinds black pepper

2 tbsp each of extra virgin olive oil and walnut or hazelnut oil

1 teasp caster sugar

4 tbsp finely snipped fresh tarragon (about 1 oz/25 g)

1 Several hours in advance, make the dressing by shaking together in a screw-top jar all the ingredients (except the tarragon) until they form an emulsion. Leave in the refrigerator.

2 About 1 hour before serving, slice the artichokes into a bowl, shake the dressing until it thickens again, add the tarragon, then pour over the artichokes.

3 Leave at room temperature until required.

TO SERVE
Arrange in a fairly shallow dish (e.g. entrée or quiche).

A Salad of Spring Leaves with a Nut Oil and Balsamic Vinegar Dressing

SERVES 6–8

Dressing keeps 1 week under refrigeration

A light and refreshing all-green salad with a high 'crunch' factor to serve with a steak or grilled chops.

1 good bulb fennel, trimmed

1 tbsp fresh lemon juice

1 small handful parsley

1 × 7 oz (200 g) pack mixed leaves, torn if necessary into bite-sized pieces

1 pack Little Gem (small hearted) lettuce, cut into wedges

1 bunch watercress, stalks removed if necessary

FOR THE DRESSING
3 fl oz (75 ml/⅓ cup) sunflower oil

1 fl oz (25 ml/2 tbsp) walnut or hazelnut oil

1 fl oz (25 ml/2 tbsp) balsamic vinegar

1 teasp lemon juice

1 teasp caster sugar or granular sweetener

1 teasp wholegrain mustard

½ teasp sea salt

5 grinds black pepper

1 small clove garlic, halved

1 To make the dressing, put all the ingredients in a large screw-top jar and shake well until thickened. Leave in the refrigerator to mature for several hours.

2 Slice the fennel (discarding the tough base) and leave in a bowl sprinkled with the lemon juice – this prevents browning and also lessens the strong flavour of aniseed.

3 Divide the parsley into sprigs.

4 An hour before the meal, mix the salad greens and drained fennel in a bowl large and wide enough to allow the contents to be later tossed with the dressing. Cover and refrigerate again until required.

TO SERVE

Shake the dressing well with the lemon juice from the fennel and pour over the salad, tossing until all the ingredients are glistening. Turn into a salad bowl.

Asparagus Salad in the Italian Style

SERVES 6–8

Serve the same day

This is a delicious way to make the most of the specially bred miniature asparagus that bridges the months until regular asparagus is in season. (That can, of course, be treated in the same way but be sure to discard any woody part of the stalk.)

24–32 miniature asparagus stalks (approx. 3 packs)

1 × 7 oz (200 g) pack crisp salad leaves (e.g. frisée)

sea salt and freshly ground black pepper

5 tbsp herb-scented olive oil (e.g. basil or herbes de Provence)

3 tbsp white wine vinegar or Champagne vinegar

1 pinch caster sugar

1 Steam or microwave the asparagus until bite tender or according to packet directions. Drain well on paper towels.

2 Arrange on individual plates or a large platter on a bed of the leaves. Season well with sea salt and black pepper.

3 Lightly whisk together the oil, vinegar and sugar, then spoon over the asparagus.

TO SERVE

Serve as an accompaniment to a main dish such as Fillets of Salmon under a Crushed Pecan Crust (see page 34) instead of a cooked vegetable.

— *Cook's Tip* —

SALADS AS ACCOMPANIMENTS

Salads, particularly ones composed of dressed vegetables (such as Asparagus Salad in the Italian Style) can of course be served instead of a hot vegetable as an accompaniment to the main course, rather than after it, but it is then important to keep the acidity of the dressing low if it is not to ruin the taste of the accompanying wine. A ratio of three to four parts of oil to one part of a mild vinegar is fine.

Herbed Tomato Chutney

SERVES 6–8

Keeps at least 1 week under refrigeration

No long cooking or maturing time is needed for this wonderful relish – the exciting blend of flavours takes only 2 hours to develop. Good with grilled steak or chops though not too assertive to serve with an oily fish dish such as grilled mackerel or herring.

2 × 14 oz (140 g) cans chopped tomatoes in concentrated tomato juice

1 large onion (8 oz/225 g), finely chopped

4 level tbsp granulated sugar

1 teasp coriander seeds

1 teasp mustard seeds

4 tbsp white wine vinegar

1 inch (2.5 cm) piece peeled fresh ginger, finely chopped

1 jalapeño (hot) pepper, seeded and finely chopped

1 teasp salt

1 tbsp chopped fresh rosemary leaves, or 1 teasp freeze-dried

1 In a heavy saucepan mix the tomatoes, onion and sugar together, and leave while you coarsely crush the coriander and mustard seeds either in a mortar or with the end of a rolling pin.

2 Add these to the pan together with all the remaining ingredients and simmer, uncovered for 10 minutes.

3 Lift out the solids with a slotted spoon and put in a bowl then simmer the liquid until it is reduced to about 4 fl oz (125 ml/½ cup).

4 Pour this liquid over the tomato mixture, stir gently and chill, covered, for at least 2 hours.

TO SERVE

Spoon into a bowl. Serve chilled with the main dish.

Spiced Kumquats

M A K E S   1   L B   (4 5 0   G)

Keep for 3 weeks under refrigeration before using

This unusual relish with the tang of the kumquats counterbalancing the sweetness of the spicy pickling solution is the perfect accompaniment to roast poultry and 'cold cuts'. The kumquats will keep as long as you let them (the high sugar content acts as a preservative).

1 lb (450 g) kumquats

1 lb (450 g/2¼ cups) granulated sugar

2 cinnamon sticks

6 cloves

4 blades mace

2 cardamom pods

8 fl oz (225 ml/1 cup) cider vinegar

1 Place the kumquats in a saucepan, barely cover with water and simmer, covered, for 10 minutes.

2 Meanwhile dissolve the sugar with the spices in the vinegar over gentle heat. Bring to the boil and cook for 5 minutes.

3 Drain the kumquats and reserve the cooking liquid. Place them in the syrup and if necessary add some of the reserved liquid to barely cover the fruit.

4 Simmer, covered, for 30 minutes. Remove from the heat and leave uncovered for 24 hours, turning in the syrup once or twice.

5 Next day bring back to the boil, drain the fruit and pack in one or two jars heated as for jam (see page 113).

6 Bring the syrup back to the boil and boil hard to thicken slightly. Pour over the kumquats with the spices. Cover and refrigerate.

T o   s e r v e

Arrange in a decorative bowl and pass round, or leave on a buffet table.

Desserts

For this section we've chosen no less than 26 'bobby-dazzlers' from our Master Class roll of honour – desserts of real distinction that will bring a meal to a luscious conclusion.

Take your pick from elegant fruit tartes, comforting baked puddings, ice cream confections or desserts that major on cream. Or for simple perfection, your choice could be a compote of fresh fruit macerated in a syrup perfumed with wine or liqueur, and accompanied by a speciality biscuit or a slice of our wonderful Chocolate and Almond Marble Cake.

TARTES, TORTEN AND STRUDEL

Fresh Berry and Cinnamon Torte

SERVES 6–8

Keeps 1 day under refrigeration. Leftovers freeze 1 month

A happy marriage between the tart fruit and the almond sponge.

oil for greasing

5 oz (150 g/⅔ cup) soft butter or margarine

5 oz (150 g/⅔ cup) caster sugar

5 oz (150 g/1¼ cups) self-raising flour

5 oz (150 g/1¼ cups) ground almonds

2 eggs

2 teasp ground cinnamon

8 oz (225 g) each of fresh or frozen raspberries and mixed summer fruits, or 1 × 1 lb (450 g) pack frozen summer fruits

1 rounded tbsp granulated sugar

2 oz (50 g/½ cup) flaked almonds

FOR THE GARNISH
1 teasp ground cinnamon

2 tbsp sieved icing sugar

Preheat the oven to Gas 4 (350°F, 180°C).

1 Lightly oil an 8½ inch (22.5 cm) spring-release cake tin.

2 In a bowl or food processor put the butter, sugar, flour, almonds, eggs and cinnamon and process or beat until a smooth but fairly heavy mixture is produced – about 30 seconds, scraping down the sides as necessary.

3 Spread half this mixture into the tin, using a fork to flatten into an even layer.

4 Arrange the chosen fruit in an even layer on top of the almond mixture and sprinkle with the granulated sugar.

5 Drop the remainder of the almond mixture in spoonfuls over the fruit. Do *not* smooth down as before.

6 Bake for 10 minutes then open the oven and quickly spread the softened dough all over the fruit then sprinkle with the almonds. Continue to cook for another 40 minutes or until the surface is firm to a gentle touch.

TO SERVE

Serve warm, dusted with the mixed cinnamon and icing sugar and accompanied by Greek yoghurt or creamy fromage frais. May be gently reheated, covered with foil.

Southern Fresh Apricot and Frangipane Flan

SERVES 8–10

Keeps 2 days under refrigeration. Leftovers freeze 1 month

A pack of ready-to-use marzipan makes an almost instant filling for this refreshing flan.

1 recipe Sweet Tarte Pastry (see page 126), or 1 × 12 oz (340 g) pack bought sweet shortcrust pastry

FOR THE FILLING
1 × 9 oz (250 g) block white marzipan or almond paste

4 oz (125 g/½ cup) unsalted butter or margarine

2 level tbsp flour

2 eggs

10 fresh apricots, halved and stoned, or 2 × 16 oz (450 g) cans choice apricots, drained

4 rounded tbsp smooth apricot jam

FOR THE GARNISH
toasted flaked almonds

Preheat the oven to Gas 4 (350°F, 180°C).

1 Roll out the dough ¼ inch (6 mm) thick, and shape and bake in a 10–11 inch (25–27.5 cm) loose-bottomed flan tin as described on page 128. (To Shape and Bake 'Blind' a Flan Case.)

2 To make the filling, break up the marzipan or almond paste into 1 inch (2.5 cm) chunks and put in the food processor with the soft butter, the flour and the eggs. Process until absolutely smooth.

3 Spread the mixture on the bottom of the pastry shell and arrange the apricot halves, cut sides down, over it.

4 Bring the jam to the boil in a small saucepan, stirring until it is melted.

5 Bake the flan for 30 minutes until the filling is puffed and feels spongy when gently touched. Let it cool on a rack then brush with the reheated jam.

TO SERVE
Place on a serving dish and scatter with almonds.

FACING PAGE 98, LEFT TO RIGHT
Croustade aux Pommes Caramalisées (page 102), *Cappuccino Souffles with Bailey's Irish Cream* (page 110)

OPPOSITE
Layered Fruits in a Lemon and Cointreau Syrup (page 111), *Toasted Almond Mocha Ice Cream Torte* (page 119)

A Tarte of Red Fruits

SERVES 6–8

Cooked tarte keeps 2 days under refrigeration. Freeze unbaked pastry case 3 months

A tarte that brings a taste of summer to the winter dinner table.

1 recipe Sweet Tarte Pastry (see page 126), or 1 × 12 oz (340 g) pack bought sweet shortcrust pastry

1 egg white

FOR THE FILLING
1 × 15 oz (425 g) can pitted dessert cherries

8 oz (225 g) fresh or frozen raspberries

3 eggs

5 fl oz (150 ml/⅔ cup) double cream

2 oz (50 g/¼ cup) caster sugar

1 teasp vanilla essence

2 oz (50 g/½ cup) ground almonds

2 tbsp eau de vie de Framboises Sauvages (wild raspberry), or Kirsch

1½ oz (40 g/3 tbsp) melted butter

1 Have ready a loose-bottomed flan tin or ceramic flan dish, 9½–10 inches (23.75–25 cm) in diameter and 1¾ inches (4 cm) deep.

2 Roll the pastry to fit the dish – there may be some pastry left over – then trim the edges neatly.

3 Prick the sides and bottom of the pastry case with a fork. Freeze for at least 30 minutes.

Meanwhile, preheat the oven to Gas 5 (375°F, 190°C).

4 Cover the pastry with foil, pressing it down carefully into shape, then bake for 20 minutes. Whisk the egg white to blend, then remove the foil and brush the pastry with the egg white. Return to the oven for 5 minutes, then cool for 10 minutes before filling.

Turn the oven down to Gas 4 (350°F, 180°C).

5 To make the filling, drain the cherries and put into a bowl with the raspberries.

6 Whisk together by hand or machine the eggs, cream, sugar, essence, ground almonds and eau de vie, then add the melted butter and stir or process until evenly mixed.

7 Arrange the fruit in the pastry case and gently pour on the custard. Bake for 40–45 minutes until the custard is set.

TO SERVE
Serve warm or at room temperature. May be reheated.

Hungarian Nüsstorte with a Compote of Mixed Berries

SERVES 8–10

Torte and compote keep 4 days under refrigeration. Torte freezes 3 months

One for the nut lover – the richness of the torte is mellowed by the sharpness of the compote.

FOR THE CRUST
2 oz (50 g/½ cup) coarsely ground walnuts

2 oz (50 g/½ cup) ground almonds

2 oz (50 g/½ cup) ground hazelnuts

1½ oz (40 g/3 tbsp) caster sugar

2 oz (50 g/¼ cup) unsalted butter, cut into 1 inch (2.5 cm) chunks

FOR THE FILLING
6 oz (175 g/1½ cups) coarsely ground walnuts

7 oz (200 g/1 cup) light brown sugar

2 eggs

1 egg yolk

4 oz (125 g/1⅓ cups) flaked or shredded coconut

2 oz (50 g/½ cup) self-raising flour

2 tbsp Crème de Framboise (raspberry), or Amaretto (almond) liqueur

FOR THE COMPOTE
1 level tbsp cornflour

5 fl oz (150 ml/⅔ cup) each of cherry syrup and red wine

1 tbsp granulated sugar

1 × 1 lb (450 g) pack frozen mixed berries, thawed

1 × 15 oz (425 g) can black or Morello cherries

2 tbsp Crème de Framboise or Amaretto

Preheat the oven to Gas 4 (350°F, 180°C).

1 First, process the coarsely ground walnuts for the crust and the filling until like fine sand. Take out the 6 oz (175 g) nuts for the filling and reserve.

2 Mix remaining walnuts for the crust with the ground almonds and hazelnuts, the sugar and butter and pulse until the mixture resembles fine crumbs. Press on the bottom and sides of an 8½–9 inch (21.25–22.5 cm) spring-form tin.

3 In a bowl beat together with a balloon whisk the brown sugar, the whole eggs and egg yolk. Stir in the reserved ground walnuts, the coconut and the flour.

4 Turn the filling into the crust and bake the torte for 40–50 minutes or until golden and set. Let the torte cool on a rack and sprinkle the top with the liqueur.

5 To make the compote put the cornflour into a small pan and slowly add the cherry syrup, wine and sugar, stirring until smooth. Bring to the boil, simmer for 3 minutes, then cool. Add the fruits and the cherries, stir in the liqueur, and chill.

TO SERVE
Serve slices of the torte with the compote and crème fraîche or ice cream.

Croustade aux Pommes Caramelisées

SERVES 6–8

Bake and serve the same day. May be refrigerated overnight or frozen for 1 month

The combination of caramelised apples, marzipan and delicate pastry make this tart irresistible. Read our advice on using filo pastry (see page 127) and all will be clear – and easy!

1 × 14 oz (140 g) pack filo pastry

3 oz (75 g/⅓ cup) unsalted butter, melted + 1 teasp for greasing

1 tbsp sugar

FOR THE FILLING
2½ lb (1.1 kg) crisp eating apples

1½ oz (40 g/3 tbsp) unsalted butter

3 oz (75 g/⅓ cup) granulated sugar

3 tbsp brandy (or rum)

4 oz (125 g) marzipan, coarsely grated

FOR THE TOPPING
2 oz (50 g/¼ cup) caster sugar

Preheat the oven to Gas 7 (425°F, 220°C).

1 For the filling, peel the apples then core and cut each into 12 wedges.

2 In a large frying pan, melt the butter and sugar together then add the apples and toss until they are softened and golden brown, sprinkling them with the brandy. Lift out the apples with a slotted spoon, boil down any remaining liquid until thick and syrupy (there will be 3–4 tbsp liquid remaining), then spoon over the apples and allow to cool.

3 Grease the inside of a round 9½–10 inch (22.5–25 cm) loose-bottomed flan tin, or a rectangular 14 × 4 inch (35.5 × 10 cm) flan tin) with the teasp butter, and dust with the sugar.

4 Take eight sheets of filo from the packet and cut into 12 inch (30 cm) squares. Lay five of these squares on top of each other, brushing each in turn with the melted butter. Lift up this stack and arrange in the flan case then trim level with the edge, forming a lower 'crust'.

5 Arrange the apples in an even layer on top and scatter with grated marzipan.

6 Now cut the remaining three sheets of filo (and any trimmings) into roughly 6 inch (15 cm) triangles, brush lightly with butter then crumple up in the hand like a chiffon scarf to make small mounds (see photo opposite page 98). Arrange these over the top of the apples, completely covering them. Sprinkle with any remaining melted butter and then with the topping caster sugar.

7 Bake for 20–25 minutes until the top is golden and the sugar has caramelised.

TO SERVE

Serve warm. May be reheated either in the oven or (carefully) under the grill, sprinkled with a little extra caster sugar.

Fresh Peach and Brandy Slice

SERVES 8 GENEROUSLY

Keeps 2 days under refrigeration. Freeze 2 months

Sun-ripened peaches, their flavour underlined by the matching liqueur, are sandwiched between layers of melt-in-the-mouth pastry.

1 recipe Rich Shortcrust Pastry for Fruit Pies (see page 126), using a whole egg and omitting the water or 1 × 12 oz (340 g) pack sweet shortcrust pastry

FOR THE FILLING
1 oz (25 g/¼ cup) ground almonds

4 oz (125 g/½ cup) sugar

1 tbsp cornflour

2 teasp finely grated lemon rind

2 lb (900 g) peaches or nectarines, sliced away from the stone

1 tbsp lemon juice

2 tbsp peach brandy

FOR THE TOPPING
the frozen pastry (see below)

2 tbsp chopped pecans or walnuts

1 tbsp golden granulated sugar

Preheat the oven to Gas 5 (375°F, 190°C) and put in a baking sheet to heat up.

1 Make the pastry as described but chill just under a half quantity and freeze the rest.

2 Roll out the chilled pastry to fit an oblong 14 × 4 inch (35 × 10 cm) or square 8 inch (20 cm) loose-bottomed flan tin. Sprinkle with the ground almonds.

3 Mix the sugar, cornflour and lemon rind in a bowl and gently fold in the slices of fruit. Turn into the prepared flan tin and sprinkle with the lemon juice and peach brandy.

4 Grate or thinly slice the frozen pastry evenly over the top and scatter with the mixed nuts and sugar.

5 Carefully lay the flan tin on the hot baking sheet and bake in the oven for 40–50 minutes or until a rich golden brown.

TO SERVE

Cut in slices and serve at room temperature, plain or with Greek yoghurt lightly sweetened with runny honey.

Marzipan and Apple Tarte

SERVES 6–8

Keeps 2 days under refrigeration

An unusual variation on the apple tart theme.

1 recipe Rich Shortcrust Pastry
for Fruit Pies (see page 126),
using a whole egg and omitting
the water

FOR THE FILLING
1 × 9 oz (250 g) pack marzipan,
chilled

4 oz (125 g/½ cup) soft butter or
margarine

2 oz (50 g/¼ cup) caster sugar

2 eggs, separated

4 large Bramley apples
(2 lb/900 g), peeled and coarsely
grated

FOR THE TOPPING
the frozen pastry (see below)

2 tbsp sugar

Preheat the oven to Gas 7 (425°F, 220°C).

1 Make the pastry as described but chill only half and freeze the remainder.

2 On a floured board roll out the chilled pastry ⅛ inch (3 mm) thick, and line the base and sides of a 10 inch (25 cm) heatproof flan dish. Cover the base with the marzipan, grated or sliced.

3 Cream the butter and sugar in a bowl until fluffy then beat in the egg yolks. Stir in the grated apples, then fold in the egg whites whisked until they hold glossy peaks. Spoon the filling into the pastry case and grate the frozen pastry on top in an even layer.

4 Scatter with the sugar and bake for 35–40 minutes until golden brown. To reheat, cover loosely with foil and leave in a moderate oven, Gas 4 (350°F, 180°C) for 20–25 minutes or until warm to the touch.

TO SERVE
Serve warm, plain or with custard sauce or frozen yoghurt.

— Cook's Tip —
GRATE PASTRY!
The higher the fat and sugar content of a pastry, the more likely it is to possess memorable melt-in-the-mouth texture. Unfortunately it is also difficult to roll out. This doesn't matter for the bottom layer – that can easily be patched. But it can be a problem for the top layer. The answer is to freeze it then grate it over the filling (see above). One of us prefers to do this by hand, the other in the food processor. The choice is yours.

Raspberry, Mango and Amaretti Strudel with Amaretto Cream

SERVES 8

Keeps 2 days under refrigeration. Freeze 1 month. Reheats well

A luscious strudel crammed with fresh fruit. (See also page 127 for information about filo pastry.)

4 oz (125 g) Amaretti biscuits

3 oz (75 g/⅜ cup) unsalted butter or block margarine

4 sheets filo pastry, measuring 12 × 18 inches (30 × 45 cm)

icing sugar

FOR THE FILLING
1 very large, well-ripened mango (1 lb/450 g total weight), peeled

8 oz (225 g) raspberries

3 tbsp caster sugar

1 tbsp fresh lemon juice

2 tbsp Amaretto (almond) or Crème de Framboises (raspberry) liqueur

FOR THE AMARETTO CREAM
1 × 7–11 oz (200–300 g) carton crème fraîche

3 tbsp Amaretto or Crème de Framboise liqueur

I Cut the mango away from the stone in slices ¼ inch (6 mm) thick, then cut in ½ inch (1.25 cm) pieces. Place in a bowl with the raspberries and sprinkle with the caster sugar, lemon juice and liqueur.
Preheat the oven to Gas 7 (425°F, 220°C).

2 Crush the biscuits with a rolling pin until like coarse sand.

3 Melt the fat in a small basin then set aside. Count out the four sheets of filo pastry then reseal the packet and return to the refrigerator or freezer.

4 On a tea towel lay the four sheets on top of each other, brushing each one with the melted fat. Scatter the crushed Amaretti biscuits over the top layer of pastry, leaving 1 inch (2.5 cm) of pastry bare of crumbs all the way round.

5 Arrange the fruit on top of the biscuits, in a mound about 2–3 inches (5–7.5 cm) wide and 3 inches (7.5 cm) from the top edge of the pastry nearest to you, leaving 1 inch (2.5 cm) of pastry clear of fruit either side. Turn the sides of the pastry in to seal in the juices then with the help of the tea towel roll up into a strudel. Place on a shallow greased baking tray, join side down.

6 Brush the top of the strudel with an even layer of the remaining fat. Make eight diagonal slashes about 2 inches (5 cm) apart through the top layer of pastry. Bake for 25–30 minutes until crisp and golden brown.

Note If juice runs out of the strudel during the baking time, simply smooth it on top of the baked pastry. It will then set into a glaze.

TO SERVE
Serve warm, sprinkled thickly with icing sugar, with Amaretto cream (the well-chilled cream mixed with the liqueur).

Hot Puddings

Upside-Down Chocolate Fudge and Pear Pudding

Serves 8

Keeps 2 days under refrigeration. Freeze 1 month

For chocaholics – the pears add a welcome fruity touch in contrast to the rich moist texture of the pudding.

2 × 15 oz (425 g) cans choice pear halves or quarters, well drained

FOR THE CAKE
1½ oz (40 g/3 tbsp) + 6 oz (175 g/¾ cup) soft butter or margarine

5 level tbsp cocoa

9 oz (250 g/1¼ cups) medium brown Muscovado sugar

3 eggs

1½ teasp vanilla essence

3 oz (75 g/¾ cup) plain flour

1 × 3½ oz (100 g/1 cup) pack walnut halves

TO PASS AT THE TABLE
brandy or eau de vie de poire

Preheat the oven to Gas 4 (350°F, 180°C).

1 Lightly oil a 9½ inch (23.75 cm) spring-form or deep cake tin and line the base with a circle of silicone paper. Arrange the well-drained fruit in concentric circles.

2 Melt the 1½ oz (40 g/3 tbsp) fat (45 seconds at 100% power in the microwave), and then stir in the cocoa and set aside.

3 Process the sugar and eggs in the food processor for 1 minute then take off the lid, add the vanilla and the 6 oz (175 g/¾ cup) fat (if used, butter should be soft) in spoonfuls together with the cocoa mixture. Put on the lid and process briefly until an even colour (scraping down the sides once). Add the flour and nuts and pulse only until evenly blended, when the nuts will be coarsely chopped.

4 Spoon the mixture carefully on top of the pears and smooth level. Bake for 40–45 minutes or until the centre is firm to a very gentle touch. To reheat, leave in baking tin, cover with foil and place in a moderate oven at Gas 4 (350°F, 180°C) until warm to the touch (do this while eating the main course).

TO SERVE

Leave the warm pudding for 5 minutes then turn out and serve with brandy or liqueur, and yoghurt, ice cream or hot custard if you wish.

Gingered Apple Upside-Down Pudding

S E R V E S 8

Keeps 3 days under refrigeration. Freeze 3 months

A spongy gingerbread is topped with apples bathed in a butterscotch sauce.

FOR THE APPLE TOPPING
2 oz (50 g/¼ cup) butter or margarine

2 oz (50 g/¼ cup) dark Muscovado sugar

1 rounded tbsp golden syrup

3 large baking apples (approx 1½ lb/675 g unpeeled weight), peeled, cored and thinly sliced on the food processor

FOR THE GINGER PUDDING
4 oz (125 g/½ cup) butter or margarine

4 oz (125 g/½ cup) soft brown sugar

6 oz (175 g/½ cup) golden syrup

1 egg

8 oz (225 g/2 cups) plain flour

2 level teasp ground ginger

½ teasp mixed sweet spice or ground cinnamon

½ teasp bicarbonate of soda dissolved in 4 fl oz (125 ml/½ cup) warm water

TO SERVE
9 oz (250 g/1 cup + 2 tbsp) creamy fromage frais or Greek yoghurt

3 pieces stem ginger, cut in little cubes

1 tbsp ginger syrup

Preheat the oven to Gas 5 (375°F, 190°C).

1 Have ready a 9 inch (22.5 cm) cake tin about 1½–2 inches (3.75–5 cm) deep.

2 Melt the apple topping fat in a pan then use a little to grease the tin.

3 Add the sugar and golden syrup to the melted fat and cook, stirring, until a rich golden brown. Mix thoroughly with the apples and place in the tin.

4 For the pudding, put the fat, sugar, syrup and egg into a bowl or food processor and beat or process until smooth. Finally add the flour sifted with the spices, alternately with the bicarbonate of soda dissolved in the water. The batter will be thin. Pour over the apples.

5 Bake for 40 minutes or until firm to the touch. Leave for 5 minutes then turn out on to a cooling rack. To reheat, leave in the tin, cover with foil and leave in a moderate oven, Gas 4 (350°F, 180°C) until heated through – about 15 minutes.

TO SERVE

Serve warm, plain or with the fromage frais or Greek yoghurt mixed with the ginger cubes and syrup.

Adam and Eve Pudding with a Calvados and Cider Sauce

SERVES 8

Keeps 3 days under refrigeration. Freeze 3 months

A light sponge pudding encloses a juicy layer of apples and crunchy sugared nuts. The sauce is made in minutes.

2 medium baking apples, peeled, cored and very thinly sliced in the food processor

FOR THE NUT MIXTURE
100 g (3½ oz/1 cup) shelled pecans, finely chopped

3 oz (75 g/¾ cup) granulated sugar

FOR THE CAKE MIXTURE
4 oz (125 g/½ cup) soft margarine

5 oz (150 g/⅔ cup) caster sugar

3 eggs

8 oz (225 g/2 cups) plain flour

1 tsp baking powder

1 teasp bicarbonate of soda

1 teasp ground cinnamon

½ teasp mixed spice

5 fl oz (150 ml/⅔ cup) strong dry cider

FOR THE SAUCE
2 egg yolks

2 oz (50 g/¼ cup) caster sugar

2 level teasp cornflour

8 fl oz (225 ml/1 cup) strong dry cider

2 tbsp Calvados or brandy

Preheat the oven to Gas 5 (375°F, 190°C).

1 Chop the nuts coarsely (most easily done in a food processor), then put with the sugar in a small bowl. Put the apples in another. Grease a tin approximately 12 × 8 × 2 inches (30 × 20 × 5 cm).

2 Cream the fat and sugar until fluffy, then beat in the eggs one at a time. Stir in the flour pre-sifted with the spices and raising agents – alternately with the liquid. Or mix in the food processor.

3 Pour half the mixture into the prepared tin, arrange the sliced apples in an even layer on top and sprinkle with half the nut mixture. Smooth the remaining cake mixture on top and sprinkle with the remaining nut mixture.

4 Bake for 35 minutes until spongy to the touch and a toothpick comes out clean from the centre.

5 To make the sauce, process all the ingredients in the food processor for 30 seconds. Turn into a 2–3 pint (1.1–1.75 litre/5–7½ cup) microwave-safe jug or bowl and cook on 100% power for 2 minutes, stirring halfway through. Cook for a further 30 seconds – it should resemble a pouring custard. If not, give it a further 30 seconds until sufficiently thickened.

6 Or, without a microwave: process all the ingredients as above and turn into a heatproof bowl that will fit over a pan one-third full of simmering water. Cook, stirring, until the mixture is thick enough to coat the back of a wooden spoon.

TO SERVE

Serve the cake warm with the sauce.

Petits Gratins aux Cerises

SERVES 6–8

Cooked gratins keep 3 days under refrigeration

A variation on the crumble theme, but dressed up for a dinner party.

FOR THE FRUIT MIXTURE
1 × 14 oz (140 g) can best black cherry pie filling

1 × 15 oz (425 g) can pitted black cherries, drained

2 tbsp cherry brandy or Kirsch

1½ tbsp lemon juice

FOR THE TOPPING
3 oz (75 g/¾ cup) plain flour

1 oz (25 g/⅓ cup) porridge oats

2½ oz (65 g/½ cup + 2 tbsp) ground almonds

4 oz (125 g/½ cup) light brown sugar

1½ teasp ground cinnamon

grated rind of ½ lemon

3 oz (75 g/⅓ cup) butter or margarine

2 oz (50 g/½ cup) nibbed almonds

Preheat the oven to Gas 5 (375°F, 190°C).

1 Lightly grease eight 5 oz (150 g) soufflé dishes and arrange on a baking sheet.

2 Mix all the ingredients for the fruit mixture gently together and divide equally between the dishes.

3 To make the topping, mix all the dry ingredients in a large bowl. Add the fat cut in small chunks and rub in lightly until the mixture is crumbly. Stir in the nibbed almonds.

4 Spread the crumble evenly on top of the cherry mixture (the dishes may be left overnight at this stage).

5 Bake for 20–25 minutes or until the top is a rich brown and crunchy.

TO SERVE

Leave to cool for 5–10 minutes then serve plain or with ice cream or crème fraîche.

Cappuccino Soufflés with Bailey's Irish Cream

SERVES 8

Serve immediately

A wondrous soufflé that can wait happily for several hours to be baked.

1 tbsp melted butter

sugar for coating the moulds

1½ oz (40 g/3 tbsp) firm butter

scant 3 oz (75 g/⅓ cup) sugar + 2 tbsp

2 oz (50 g/½ cup) strong white flour

1 oz (25 g/¼ cup) cocoa powder

10 fl oz (275 ml/1¼ cups) milk

2 sachets (1 level tbsp) instant espresso coffee

1½–2 teasp vanilla essence

5 eggs, separated, at room temperature

FOR DUSTING
sifted icing sugar

TO SERVE
Bailey's Irish Cream Liqueur

Note   The soufflé mixture can be prepared and portioned 3–4 hours ahead, then left at room temperature (preferably cool) to pop into the oven as the main course dishes are cleared away.

1 Paint eight ramekins (individual soufflé dishes) about 3½ inches (8.75 cm) wide and 1½ inches (2.75 cm) deep with the melted butter; coat generously with sugar. Chill.

Preheat the oven to Gas 6 (400°F, 200°C).

2 Combine the firm butter, the 3 oz (75 g/⅓ cup) sugar, the flour and cocoa powder in a food processor; whirl to form a crumbly mixture.

3 Bring the milk and coffee powder to the boil in a medium saucepan, stirring. Whisk in the cocoa mixture. Return to the boil, stirring, then remove from the heat. Stir in the vanilla essence, then whisk in the egg yolks one at a time.

4 Whisk the egg whites until soft peaks form, then whisk in the 2 tbsp sugar and whisk again until stiff. Stir one-quarter of the whites into the warm cocoa mixture to lighten it. Gently fold in the remainder. Divide the mixture between the ramekins, almost filling them.

5 Set the moulds on kitchen paper or a J cloth in a roasting pan (the dishes may be left 3–4 hours at this point). Pour in boiling water to reach halfway up the sides of the moulds. Set in the centre of the oven and bake for 17–20 minutes, until the centre no longer seems liquid – but not baked firm.

TO SERVE

Dredge with icing sugar and serve at once with the liqueur. Each guest can spoon 1–2 tbsp into the centre of their soufflé.

RATHER SPECIAL FRUIT COMPOTES

Layered Fruits in a Lemon and Cointreau Syrup

SERVES 8

Compote of mangoes keeps 48 hours under refrigeration

A simple but eye-catching presentation with the accent on the glorious flavours of the choice fruits accentuated by the liqueur. The flavour and texture of the mango is improved if it's allowed to macerate in the syrup overnight.

2 large ripe mangoes

1 lb (450 g/2¾ cups) fresh strawberries

8 oz (225 g/1½ cups) fresh redcurrants, blueberries or raspberries

FOR THE SYRUP
3 tbsp caster sugar

3 tbsp lemon juice

2 tbsp Cointreau (or other orange-flavoured liqueur)

FOR THE GARNISH
8 sprigs fresh chervil or shreds of lemon zest

Make sure the mangoes are fully ripe – they should give slightly all over to gentle pressure.

1 Peel the mangoes and cut the flesh away from the stone then cut into pieces the size of a strawberry slice.

2 For the syrup, heat the sugar and lemon juice until dissolved (30 seconds in the microwave), then stir in the liqueur.

3 Pour the syrup over the mango slices and refrigerate.

4 The next day, hull and slice the strawberries.

5 In wine glasses, arrange layers of the three fruits then spoon over the liqueur syrup. Chill until required.

TO SERVE

Garnish with tiny sprigs of chervil or the shreds of lemon zest.

Kumquats in Cognac

FILLS 1 × 2 LB (900 G) JAR

Keeps 6 months under refrigeration

These are easy to prepare (albeit over 2 days), but they are utterly delicious – wonderful to serve with fromage frais, over icecream or to add to a fruit salad. You don't need to raid the drinks cabinet for VSOP cognac – an own-brand from the supermarket will do fine.

1½ lb (675 g) kumquats	8 fl oz (225 ml/1 cup) water
1 lb (450 g/2¼ cups) sugar	6 fl oz (175 ml/¾ cup) cognac

1 Place the washed kumquats in a saucepan, barely cover with water and bring to the boil, then simmer covered for 10 minutes. Drain and reserve the cooking liquid.

2 In the same pan, dissolve the sugar in the 8 fl oz (225 ml/1 cup) water over medium heat, stirring, then bring to the boil and cook for 5 minutes.

3 Add the kumquats and, if necessary, enough of the reserved cooking liquid barely to cover the fruit. Simmer covered for 30 minutes. Remove from the heat and leave uncovered for 24 hours, turning in the syrup once or twice.

4 Next day, bring back to the boil, drain the fruit and pack in a heated jar (or jars) (see opposite) large enough to hold them plus 12 fl oz (350 ml/1½ cups) of the cognac syrup.

5 Bring the syrup back to the boil and boil hard until almost viscous – like heavy syrup in canned fruit. Do not, however, allow it to change colour (the start of caramelisation) or the flavour will be spoilt.

6 Measure the syrup – there should be about 6 fl oz (175 ml/¾ cup), add an equal amount of cognac then pour over the fruit and seal tightly. Refrigerate when cold. Use after 3 weeks.

Note   Leftover syrup will keep indefinitely in the refrigerator and can be added to a fresh fruit salad.

Dried Apricots in Amaretto

FILLS 2 × 1 LB (450 G) JARS

Keeps 3 months under refrigeration

Wonderful store-cupboard insurance against unexpected guests. Serve with a luxury vanilla icecream or frozen yoghurt, and you're in business!

1 lb (450 g/3 cups) dried ready-to-eat apricots

4 oz (125 g/½ cup) sugar

2 strips orange zest

2 strips lemon zest

4 oz (125 g/1 cup) split blanched almonds

5 fl oz (150 ml/⅔ cup) Amaretto or other almond-flavoured liqueur

1 Put the apricots, sugar, orange and lemon zest into a pan with 1¾ pints (1 litre/4 cups) water. Bring slowly to the boil, stirring occasionally, to dissolve the sugar. Simmer uncovered for 10 minutes to thicken the syrup.

2 Reduce the heat and simmer the fruit, covered, for 30 minutes. Drain and reserve the syrup. Allow the fruit to cool.

3 Pack the apricots and almonds into two sterilised warm jars (see below). Divide the Amaretto between the jars then fill up with the reserved syrup. Tightly close the jars and reverse them gently to mix the liquids together.

4 Leave the jars right side up in a cool dry place to mature for 2 weeks.

— *Cook's Tip* —

TO STERILISE PRESERVING JARS

For convenience, select jars that have a built-in rubber closure in the lid. This avoids having to use the old-fashioned method of greaseproof discs and covers held in place with rubber bands.

First thoroughly wash both the jars and their lids in hot detergent then rinse well and drain. Next sterilise the jars using one of the following methods:

In a conventional oven: Place the jars upside down, together with their lids, in a low oven (Gas ½/250°F/120°C)) for 10 minutes or until they are very hot to the touch.

In a microwave oven: Quarter fill each jar with cold water then leave in the oven on 100% power until the water boils – about 1½ to 2½ minutes according to the number and size of the jars. Take out and leave upside down on kitchen paper to drain and dry.

Using either method, fill the jars with preserve when they are hot from the oven.

Pears Poached in Red Wine and Crème de Cassis

S E R V E S 6 – 8

Fruit keeps 3 days under refrigeration. Freeze 6 months

The combination of the wine-soaked pears served with a wedge of Brie-type creamy cheese is unusual – and quite delectable. The cheese called Henri IV makes the perfect match.

6–8 small firm Conference pears

1 × 9 fl oz (250 ml) can or 8 fl oz (225 ml/1 cup) fruity red wine

3 oz (75 g/⅓ cup) granulated sugar

2 pieces thinly pared orange rind

2 pieces thinly pared lemon rind

1 cinnamon stick

4 cloves

1 tbsp lemon juice

2 teasp cornflour or arrowroot mixed with 4 tbsp Crème de Cassis (blackcurrant liqueur)

T O S E R V E
1–1½ oz (25–40 g) Henri IV or other Brie-type, semi-soft cheese per person

1 Peel the pears but leave them whole. Cut a tiny slice from the base of each so they will stand evenly in the serving dish.

2 Choose a lidded pan large enough to hold the pears lying flat on the bottom (a 10 inch/25 cm sauté pan, for instance). Put in the wine, sugar, rinds, spices and lemon juice, and heat gently until the sugar dissolves, stirring all the time.

3 Add the pears, bring to the boil, cover and simmer very gently, turning once or twice until the fruit feels just tender when pierced with a sharp pointed knife. This will take about 30 minutes for very hard pears, but start testing after 20. By this time the pears will be a beautiful pink colour. Take out and put on a plate using a draining spoon.

4 Bring the cooking liquid back to the boil, then bubble until it has a syrupy consistency with a pleasing 'winey' flavour.

5 Stir in the cornflour (or arrowroot) mixed smooth with the Crème de Cassis, bubble until clear, then strain over the fruit. Chill well, turning the pears occasionally.

T O S E R V E
Arrange a pear with a little of the syrup spooned over, on each dessert plate, with a wedge of cheese and a couple of digestive or oat biscuits.

Scented Fruits with a Vanilla and Orange Fromage Frais

SERVES 6–8

Serve the same day

A refreshing dessert for a hot summer's evening. Good for the low-fat brigade!

1 oz (25 g/2 tbsp) caster sugar

5 fl oz (150 ml/⅔ cup) Muscat dessert wine (e.g. Beaumes de Venise)

1 tbsp lemon juice

2 tbsp orange-blossom water or fresh orange juice

1 lb (450 g/2¾ cups) berries (e.g. raspberries, strawberries, tayberries, blueberries)

8 oz (225 g) kumquats

4 fresh figs, cut in sixths

2 oz (50 g/½ cup) shelled natural pistachios, coarsely chopped

FOR THE FROMAGE FRAIS
10 fl oz (275 ml/1¼ cups) vanilla-flavoured fromage frais

3 teasp finely grated orange rind

2 tbsp orange liqueur (e.g. Curaçao, Cointreau, Grand Marnier)

1 Put the caster sugar in a saucepan with the wine. Heat slowly and stir until the sugar has dissolved, then bring to the boil and boil rapidly for 1 minute. Allow the syrup to cool slightly then stir in the lemon juice and orange-blossom water. Cool completely then chill until required.

2 Place the chosen berries (cut the strawberries, if used, lengthways in four) in a serving dish with the kumquats and figs and pour over the cold syrup. Mix well and chill in the refrigerator for about 1 hour.

3 Mix the fromage frais with the orange rind and liqueur, then spoon into a serving jug or bowl and chill well.

TO SERVE

Divide the fruit and syrup into stemmed wine glasses or a compotier and top with the nuts. Pass the fromage frais.

Nectarines in White Wine with Peppercorns, Passion Fruit and Toasted Pecans

SERVES 8

Serve after 24 hours. May be refrigerated for up to 4 days

A simple but sophisticated presentation with the peppercorns pointing up the flavour of the fruit.

8–10 large, choice nectarines (or peaches)

FOR THE POACHING SYRUP
1 level tbsp mixed-colour peppercorns

10 fl oz (275 ml/1¼ cups) white wine (or 1 × 9 fl oz/250 ml can)

5 fl oz (150 ml/⅔ cup) water

4 oz (125 g/½ cup) granulated sugar

1 cinnamon stick

FOR THE GARNISH
4 tbsp (approx. 2 oz/50 g/½ cup) pecan halves, lightly toasted in a non-stick frying pan

seeds from 2 passion fruit

1 The day before, poach the fruit. First, tie the peppercorns in a square of muslin or a light-coloured J cloth, and lightly crush, either in a mortar or with the end of a rolling pin.

2 Put in a shallow lidded pan wide enough to hold the peaches in one layer, together with the wine, water, sugar and cinnamon stick.

3 Bring to the boil, stirring constantly, then add the washed nectarines. Baste with the liquid, cover and poach for 5–8 minutes until barely tender when pierced with a slim knife. Cover and leave off the heat to steam for 15 minutes.

4 Lift the fruit out of the syrup with a slotted spoon and peel and discard the skins. Place the fruit in a wide lidded container.

5 Bring the syrup back to the boil and simmer for 5 minutes or until the flavour has intensified. Discard the peppercorns but leave in the cinnamon stick.

6 Pour the syrup over and around the fruit, then cover and chill overnight, turning the fruit once or twice.

TO SERVE

Arrange the peaches on one large serving dish or individual bowls or plates. Divide the syrup between them, then scatter with the pecan halves and passion fruit seeds.

COLD AND FROZEN DESSERTS

Spiced Cider Syllabub with Poached Pears

SERVES 8

Keeps 2 days under refrigeration

A light, elegant dessert to serve after a hearty main course.

4 medium Conference pears, peeled, cored and halved

10 fl oz (275 ml/1¼ cups) dry cider

5 fl oz (150 ml/⅔ cup) white wine

3 oz (75 g/⅓ cup) caster sugar

1 tbsp dark brown Muscovado sugar

1 cinnamon stick

6 cloves

2 tbsp lemon juice

finely grated zest of ½ lemon

FOR THE SYLLABUB
15 fl oz (425 ml/2 cups) double cream, or 12 fl oz (350 ml/1½ cups) non-dairy cream

the pear cooking liquor reduced to 8 fl oz (225 ml/1 cup)

FOR THE GARNISH
icing sugar mixed with a little ground cinnamon

I The day before, put the cider and wine into a wide-based pan (preferably enamelled or stainless steel), and add the sugar and spices with half the lemon juice. Bring to the boil. Add the halved pears, baste well, cover and simmer until tender but not mushy – 10–15 minutes. Test by piercing with a sharp knife.

2 Lift out the pears and put into a bowl then boil the liquid down until it measures 8 fl oz (225 ml/1 cup). Pour this syrup over the fruit, add the lemon rind and remaining lemon juice, and refrigerate overnight.

3 The next day, lift out the pears with a slotted spoon, and cut into slices. Divide between eight large wine glasses – a half pear to a glass.

4 To make the syllabub, whip the cream until it hangs on the whisk, then gradually whisk in the strained syrup, whipping continuously until the mixture holds soft peaks. Spoon or pipe on top of the fruit and chill for at least 1½–2 hours.

TO SERVE
Sprinkle with the cinnamon sugar and pass a dish of crisp biscuits – e.g. *langue de chat.*

Frozen Parfait Rothschild

SERVES 8

Freezes 3 months

One of the simplest ice creams we know, with a 'soft scoop' texture and the flavour of fruit brandy in every spoonful. Instead of making the meringues yourself, you could use twelve bought meringues.

FOR THE GOLDEN MERINGUES	FOR THE FLAVOURED CREAM
2 egg whites	10 fl oz (275 ml/1¼ cups) double cream
¼ teasp cream of tartar	4 tbsp Kirsch
4 oz (125 g/½ cup) golden caster sugar	4 oz (125 g/½ cup) mixed glacé fruit, finely chopped (e.g. pineapple, mixed cherries, ginger)
1 teasp cornflour	½ teasp vanilla essence

Preheat the oven to Gas 2 (300°F, 150°C).

1 First make the meringues. Put the egg whites and cream of tartar into a mixing bowl. Mix together the sugar and cornflour. Whisk the whites until they hold floppy peaks then add the sugar a tablespoonful at a time, whisking until stiff after each addition – the meringue should now stand in stiff peaks.

2 With a spoon, shape into 2 inch (5 cm) meringues on a baking sheet lined with silicone paper, leaving 2 inches (5 cm) between them.

3 Put the meringues into the oven and immediately turn the temperature down to Gas 1 (275°F, 140°C). Bake for 1 hour until crisp right through and easy to lift off the paper. Allow to go quite cold then break into roughly 1 inch (2.5 cm) pieces. Break up the bought meringues (if using) in the same way.

4 Whip the cream to the soft peak stage then whisk in the liqueur until stiff. Fold in the glacé fruit and the broken meringues.

5 Spoon into small pots or one slim 2 lb (900 g) loaf tin lined with silicone paper, and freeze for at least 24 hours before serving.

TO SERVE

Serve the little pots straight from the freezer with a crisp biscuit or bought petit four. Again, straight from the freezer, turn the loaf tin out on to a long slim platter. Decorate with fresh fruit in season – little bunches of cherries or grapes, physalis or fresh pineapple, all lightly dusted with icing sugar.

Toasted Almond Mocha Ice Cream Torte

SERVES 8–10

Freeze for 3 months

Here's an 'assembly job' based on ready-to-serve ice cream customised with lovely additional ingredients such as chocolate, nuts and liqueur.

FOR THE TORTE CASE
4 oz (125 g/1 cup) blanched almonds

6 oz (175 g) chocolate digestive biscuits (about 10), frozen for at least 30 minutes

2 oz (50 g/¼ cup) unsalted butter, melted

FOR THE FILLING
6 oz (175 g/1½ cups) blanched almonds

4 tbsp Amaretto (almond) liqueur

1 litre (1¾) pints coffee or chocolate ice cream, slightly softened

4 oz (125 g) plain dessert chocolate, finely chopped, or 4 oz (125 g) best-quality chocolate drops

FOR THE TOPPING
1 oz (25 g/¼ cup) ready-toasted flaked almonds

1 oz (25 g) chocolate, shredded with a potato peeler

1 Have ready a 9½ inch (23.75 cm) flan tin with a removable base.

2 First very coarsely chop all the almonds – those for the torte case, plus those for the filling – and toss in a non-stick pan until lightly coloured. Weigh out the 6 oz (175 g/1½ cups) for the filling and leave to cool.

3 Process the remaining toasted almonds until finely ground. Turn into a bowl. Now process the frozen digestives until crumbed. Add to the ground almonds with the melted butter and stir until evenly moistened then spoon into the flan tin and pat firmly on to the base and sides. Freeze for 30 minutes.

4 To make the filling, process the 6 oz (175 g) toasted almonds until the consistency of a nut butter, scraping the sides down occasionally, then process with the Amaretto for 3 seconds.

5 Add the icecream, broken into chunks if necessary, and the chocolate, and pulse six or eight times until the filling is smooth and well combined.

6 Spoon into the frozen crust, spreading it into an even layer. Scatter the mixed flaked almonds and chocolate on top, and freeze overnight.

Note If the torte is to be kept in the freezer more than 24 hours, cover it with clingfilm when firm.

TO SERVE

Unmould the torte from the tin, place on a serving dish then leave in the freezer. Allow to stand at room temperature during the main course, then cut in sections.

Coffee and Burnt Almond Frozen Parfait with a Dark Chocolate Sauce

SERVES 10–12

Freeze 1 month

A spectacular dessert for a buffet meal.

FOR THE ICE CREAM
3 eggs, separated

1 pinch salt

3 oz (75 g/½ cup) icing sugar

3 tbsp instant espresso coffee dissolved in 1½ tbsp boiling water

3–4 oz (75–125 g/¾–1 cup) nibbed almonds toasted in a moderate oven until a rich brown

8 fl oz (225 ml/1 cup) whipping or non-dairy cream

FOR THE AMARETTI CREAM TOPPING
7 fl oz (200 ml/¾ cup + 2 tbsp) whipping or non-dairy cream

5–6 oz (150–175 g) Amaretti or ratafia biscuits

FOR THE SAUCE
6 oz (175 g) plain chocolate

2 oz (50 g/¼ cup) sugar

5 fl oz (150 ml/⅔ cup) water

1 oz (25 g/2 tbsp) butter or margarine

1 teasp vanilla essence

I Use a 9 inch (22.5 cm) spring-form tin or a loaf tin about 11–12 inches (27.5–30 cm) long. Line the base of the chosen tin with silicone paper.

2 To make the ice cream whisk the egg whites with the salt until they hold floppy peaks then whisk in the icing sugar a tablespoon at a time, whisking until stiff after each addition. Gently whisk in the egg yolks until the colour is even then fold in the cooled liquid coffee and the nuts.

3 Whip the cream to soft peaks, then fold into the egg white mixture gently. Turn into the chosen container and freeze for 1 hour.

4 To make the Amaretti cream topping, whisk the cream until it holds its shape then fold in the biscuits (which have been roughly crushed with a rolling pin in a plastic bag). Smooth on top of the partly frozen parfait and continue to freeze for at least 4 hours or until firm.

5 Before dinner, carefully turn the ice cream out on to a tray then turn over on to a serving dish. Return to the freezer. Take out during the main course.

6 The chocolate sauce can be made early in the day. Put the broken-up chocolate, the sugar and the water into a small pan and bring slowly to the boil, then simmer for 5 minutes or until of coating consistency. Stir in the fat and vanilla essence.

TO SERVE
Serve the parfait in slices or wedges with the warm or cold chocolate sauce.

Iced Chocolate and Caramelised Hazelnut Terrine

SERVES 12–15

The icecream will freeze for 1 month

A little culinary sleight of hand transforms a litre of ice cream into a very special frozen dessert!

1 litre (1¾ pints) luxury vanilla icecream

FOR THE NUT CRUNCH
2 rounded tbsp golden syrup

1½ oz (40 g/3 tbsp) butter or margarine

4 oz (125 g/½ cup) light brown sugar

4 oz (125 g/1 cup) shelled hazelnuts

FOR THE CRUMB MIXTURE
10 chocolate digestive biscuits, frozen for 15 minutes then crumbed in the food processor

2 oz (50 g/¼ cup) melted butter or margarine

1 level tbsp icing sugar

FOR THE GARNISH
clusters of seedless black grapes and physalis (Cape gooseberries)

1 To make the nut crunch, put the golden syrup, butter or margarine and sugar in a heavy saucepan and stir over gentle heat until melted. Add the nuts. Turn up the heat and continue stirring until the mixture is a rich golden brown. Immediately pour into a small baking tin lined with silicone paper.

2 As soon as the nut crunch is set hard, break it up into approximately 1 inch (2.5 cm) chunks and process in the food processor until a coarse powder.

3 Turn the ice cream into a bowl. (Depending on the texture, it may first need to be softened at room temperature.) Stir in the nut crunch.

4 Line a deep ice tray or a long plastic container measuring about 11 × 4 × 1½ inches (27.5 × 10 × 3.75 cm) with a strip of silicone paper, extending it above the top of the container.

5 Combine all the crumb mixture ingredients. Sprinkle two-thirds of this mixture on to the silicone paper in the container, then cover with the ice cream. Cover with the remaining crumbs. Freeze until firm (about 2–3 hours).

TO SERVE

Run a knife around the edge of the tin, reverse a long serving plate on top, then carefully turn out the terrine. Remove the paper and re-freeze until required. Just before serving, decorate with the fruit.

Meringues Mont Blancs

MAKES 10–12

Keep 2 days under refrigeration. Freeze filled cups (or filling alone) 3 months

Using the natural purée rather than crème de marrons allows the true flavour of the chestnuts to come through loud and clear. You can use bought or home-made meringue cups, about 2½ inches (6.25 cm) across: you need twelve. For an alternative presentation, use to fill a 4-egg white 8 inch (20 cm) pavlova (two layers), or to fill tiny little meringue 'seashells'.

FOR HOME-MADE MERINGUES
3 egg whites

¼ teasp cream of tartar

1½ teasp cornflour

6 oz (175 g/¾ cup) caster sugar

FOR THE FILLING
1 can unsweetened chestnut purée (approx. 425 g/15 oz)

4 tbsp brandy or rum, or chocolate or coffee-flavoured liqueur (e.g. Sabra, Tia Maria, Bailey's Irish Cream)

4 oz (125 g/⅔ cup) icing sugar

10 fl oz (275 ml/1¼ cup) whipping or double cream

FOR THE TOPPING
2 oz (50 g) plain chocolate, melted

Preheat the oven to Gas 2 (300°F, 150°C). Line a large baking tray with silicone paper.

1 For the meringues, whisk the whites with the cream of tartar until they hold floppy peaks. Mix the cornflour with the sugar then add a tbsp at a time to the egg whites, whisking until stiff after each addition.

2 Put a ½ inch (1.25 cm) coarse rose or plain tube into a large piping bag and fill two-thirds full with the meringue mixture. Starting from the centre of the base, pipe out little cups about 2½ inches (6.25 cm) across, on to the baking sheet. The cups will expand in the oven, so leave 2 inches (5 cm) between them.

3 Put the trays of meringues into the oven, then immediately turn the temperature down to Gas 1 (275°F, 140°C). Bake for 1 hour or until the cups feel crisp to the touch and lift off the tray easily. Put on cooling racks. Store unfilled cases at room temperature in airtight plastic containers.

4 For the filling, process the chestnut purée, alcohol and sugar in the food processor until smooth and creamy (taste and add extra sugar if required). Whip the cream until it holds peaks then fold in the chestnut mixture. Pipe in a tall spiral into each meringue cup.

5 Drizzle the melted chocolate over each cup. Chill or freeze until required.

TO SERVE

Serve cold but not frozen.

Chocolate and Almond Marble Cake

SERVES 6–8

Keeps 1 week in an airtight container. Freeze 6 months

The ground almonds added to the traditional recipe give this glorious Viennese cake a moist yet delicate texture. We have adapted the preparation method for the food processor with spectacularly good results. However it can be made by the conventional creaming method or one-stage method (see below). Wonderful with coffee or a glass of wine.

4 large eggs

8 oz (225 g/1 cup) caster sugar

8 oz (225/1 cup) soft butter or margarine

3 oz (75 g/¾ cup) ground almonds

5 oz (150 g/1¼ cups) supreme sponge self-raising flour

2 level tbsp cocoa

3 tbsp drinking chocolate

1 teasp vanilla essence

Preheat the oven to Gas 4 (350°F, 180°C). Grease a 9–10 inch (23½–25 cm) kugelhüpf or ring tin, or an 8 inch (20 cm) square tin, 2–3 inches (5–7 cm) deep.

1 To mix by food processor, process the eggs and the sugar for 1½ minutes until thickened and lighter in colour, scraping the sides down after 45 seconds.

2 Add the soft butter or margarine, then process until the mixture resembles mayonnaise – about 10 seconds.

3 Put the ground almonds and flour on top and pulse until evenly blended with the first mixture, scraping the sides down once.

4 Spoon half the mixture, by the tablespoon, into the chosen tin, leaving gaps between the spoonfuls.

5 Add the cocoa, drinking chocolate and the vanilla essence to the remaining mixture and pulse until evenly blended.

6 Spoon the chocolate mixture into the gaps in the plain mixture, then level the top.

7 Bake for approximately 45 minutes, or until the cake has shrunk from the sides of the tin and the centre springs back when gently pressed.

8 Turn upside down on a cooling tray and leave for 15 minutes, then gently ease out of the tin.

Note To mix by hand or with an electric mixer (the one-stage method), put all the ingredients except the cocoa, drinking chocolate and vanilla essence into a bowl and beat until smooth and creamy – about 3 minutes. Continue from stage 4, as in the food processor method above.

TO SERVE

Serve sprinkled with icing sugar.

Pastry Basics

You can forget the traditional advice about 'cool hands' when you make pastry in the food processor using our method. Follow our advice and your pastry will have a melt-in-the-mouth texture yet never stick to the board.

However, when time is of the essence, it's worth keeping a stock of commercial packs in the freezer. There are excellent ready-to-roll – and in some cases ready-rolled – pastries to be found, both chilled and frozen, in every supermarket and speciality food shop, with new and improved ones constantly being developed. Varieties presently on the market include shortcrust, sweet shortcrust, puff and filo. Factory-made filo, strudel and puff pastry are actually superior to all but the finest home-made. For the weekend cook, we don't think making your own versions of these is a sensible option.

However, any of the other 'made from scratch' versions we give below will reward you with a bonus of superior flavour and texture. We have vastly simplified pastry-making by using a method we have developed for the food processor, which makes it easy for even a novice cook to produce perfect pastry every time.

Food Processor Method for Mixing Pastry

To make successful pastry with a food processor, it is best to process both the dry and the liquid ingredients at the same time and to stop processing at the moist 'crumb' stage. This prevents the fat being rubbed in too finely which can make the pastry very difficult to roll out. Our method produces a lovely short pastry that is very easy to handle.

Use the metal blade and put the dry ingredients and the well-chilled fat (cut into 1 inch/2.5 cm chunks) into the bowl. Mix together the liquid ingredients to blend (including eggs if used), then turn on the machine and pour them down the feed tube, pulsing only until the mixture looks like a very moist crumble. Tip it into a bowl and gather together into a dough.

Turn the pastry on to a board or counter-top sprinkled with a very light layer of flour. Knead it gently with the fingertips to remove any cracks, flatten into a 1 inch (2.5 cm) disc, wrap in foil or clingfilm and chill in the refrigerator for at least half an hour. (At this stage it can be frozen for up to 3 months, or refrigerated for 2 days.)

Note   Chilling pastry has two purposes: it 'relaxes' the dough after the mixing process which will have made it somewhat 'elastic' and therefore liable to shrink in the oven; and it firms up the fat content, making the dough easier to roll out.

Savoury Tart Pastry

S U F F I C I E N T   F O R   1   ×   8 – 9   I N C H   (2 0 – 2 2   C M)   F L A N   C A S E

Uncooked pastry keeps 2 days under refrigeration. Freeze 3 months

This is splendid for all kinds of quiches or savoury tarts.

6 oz (175 g/1½ cups) plain flour

1 pinch salt

1 level teasp icing sugar

4 oz (125 g/½ cup) cold butter or block (baking) margarine, diced

2 tbsp icy water

1 squeeze lemon juice

Make as described above.

Brown Herb Pastry

SUFFICIENT FOR 1 × 9–12 INCH (22.5–30 CM) QUICHE OR TART TIN

Uncooked pastry keeps 2 days under refrigeration. Freeze 3 months

A very flavourful pastry.

4 oz (125 g/1 cup) granary or plain brown flour

4 oz (125 g/1 cup) plain white flour

½ teasp salt

2 teasp icing sugar

1 teasp freeze-dried herbes de Provence

1 teasp freeze-dried fines herbes

1 rounded tbsp chopped fresh or frozen parsley

1 teasp dry mustard

5 oz (150 g/⅔ cup) butter or block (baking) margarine, diced

1 egg, beaten with 1 teasp wine vinegar and 1 tbsp cold water

Make as described on page 125.

VARIATION

Omit the herbs and stir in 1 teasp mild curry powder.

Rich Shortcrust Pastry for Fruit Pies

SUFFICIENT FOR A TWO-CRUST SHALLOW PLATE PIE 10 INCHES (25 CM) IN DIAMETER, OR AN 8–9 INCH (20–22.5 CM) PIE 1 INCH (2.5 CM) DEEP

Raw pastry keeps 2 days under refrigeration. Freeze 3 months

A tender, slightly flaky pastry.

6 oz (175 g/1½ cups) plain flour

1 pinch salt

1 level teasp icing sugar

4 oz (125 g/½ cup) cold butter or block (baking) margarine, diced

2 tbsp icy water

1 squeeze lemon juice

Make as described on page 125.

Sweet Tarte Pastry

SUFFICIENT FOR 1 × 9–12 INCH (22.5–30 CM) TARTE TIN

*Unbaked pastry keeps 1 day under refrigeration. Freeze raw 1 month,
cooked case 3 months*

A crisp melt-in-the-mouth pastry. The use of icing instead of caster sugar ensures that the pastry keeps its shape even when baked 'blind'.

8 oz (225 g/2 cups) plain flour

1 pinch salt

2 oz (50 g/⅓ cup) icing sugar

5 oz (150 g/⅔ cup) butter or block (baking) margarine, diced

2 egg yolks

Make as described on page 125.

Note Because this pastry is only bound together with egg yolks it is more like a biscuit dough and can therefore be processed longer than the other pastries – that is until the ingredients are beginning to cling together in small balls. Turn it out as before and knead until quite free of cracks and with a plasticine-like texture. Chill as before.

Filo and Strudel Pastry

As they are made in a very similar way and with identical ingredients, they are for all practical purposes completely interchangeable (strudel pastry is slightly thicker). Some makes are sold chilled, others frozen. Conditions for storing and defrosting (if necessary) are generally printed on the box.

The size of the sheets varies from one brand to another. If necessary, sheets can be enlarged by overlapping them to produce the correct shape.

WHEN IT'S IN GOOD CONDITION

Each sheet will feel slightly moist and can be screwed up in the hand like tissue paper without cracking or breaking. But if it feels dry and brittle the moment you take it from the pack, or if some of the layers are 'glued together', then it's probably been subjected to fluctuations in temperature before you bought it; it will be most unsatisfactory to use so take it back to the shop and get it replaced. Don't worry about the white powder that can be seen between the sheets, however – this is only a dusting of cornflour used to stop them sticking together.

PROTECTING THE PASTRY FROM THE AIR

As it contains only a tiny amount of vegetable oil or fat, filo pastry starts to dry out the moment it is exposed to the air. As soon as you take any of the sheets from the packet, put them under a tea towel and keep them there until you're ready to brush them with a protective layer of fat.

The role of fat

This produces the wonderful flakiness for which this pastry is famed, as well as stopping the sheets of pastry from drying out. You can use unsalted butter or margarine or (for some savoury dishes) oil. Any salt present in the fat that is brushed on will make the pastry brown unevenly, so if you cannot get any unsalted fat and have to use a salted butter or margarine, be sure to discard any of the residue that sinks to the bottom after it has been melted.

The amount of fat

You will need far less than you think – just enough to coat each sheet of pastry with a very thin layer. Use a pastry brush to do this, wielding it as though applying a coat of paint, and removing any puddles of fat from the surface of the sheet. If the fat is applied sparingly in this way you can achieve a result similar to puff pastry, but using only half the quantity of fat. However, it is absolutely essential to brush every surface of the pastry that is exposed to the air, particularly if it is not to be cooked at once, but stored in the freezer or the refrigerator.

To Shape and Bake 'Blind' a Pastry Case

Roll out the chilled dough ⅛ inch (3 mm) thick and carefully ease it into the chosen tin, taking a little 'tuck' in it all the way round the bottom edge of the tin so that the case is slightly thicker near the bottom than it is at the top (this is to prevent shrinkage). Roll the rolling pin over the top edge of the case to remove excess pastry.

Prick the bottom and the sides of the case with a fork held at a slight angle, then press a large piece of foil into its shape, completely covering the bottom and sides of the pastry. Freeze for 1 hour.

Preheat the oven to Gas 5 (375°F, 190°C), and bake the pastry case for 10 minutes. Carefully remove the foil, re-prick the case it if looks puffy and return to the oven for a further 10 minutes or until a pale gold in colour. Cool on a rack.

Some recipes may indicate a slightly different baking method.

Index